A Story of Faith and Family

from STREET LIGHTS *to* STARS

BECKY MCGURRIN

ISBN-13: 978-1-932676-28-0
ISBN-10: 1-932676-28-7
Printed in the United States of America

Layout & Cover Design: Lanette Steiner

All Scriptures taken from the King James Version
unless otherwise indicated.

For information regarding bulk purchases, please contact:
Vision Publishers orders at 1-877-488-0901
Vision Publishers at P.O. Box 190, Harrisonburg, VA 22803

For information or comment, write to:
Vision Publishers
P.O. Box 190
Harrisonburg, VA 22803
Phone: 877-488-0901
Fax: 540-437-1969
E-mail: orders@vision-publishers.com
www.vision-publishers.com
(see order form in back)

P.O. Box 190
Harrisonburg, VA 22803

CONTENTS

FOREWORD

I SAT IN A doctor's waiting room a few years ago pretending to not notice the man who was staring at me from across the room. It was one of those years when "Amish" novels were hot sellers, so I had a pretty good guess as to what he was thinking. My cape dress and mesh head covering did make me rather conspicuous.

"Ma'am?" he asked when I finally looked over at him and smiled.

"Ma'am, do you know what college is?"

It was hard not to let out a giggle. "Yes. I've been to college." He looked surprised.

"Do you know what biology is?" I suppressed another giggle and answered, "Yes, I had to study a bit of biology to get my degree in Chemistry Education."

The poor fellow looked like I had just told him that they were selling babies, two for a dollar, at the local hardware store.

We spent the rest of a good hour talking together about biology and poetry and the incredible beauty of the Psalms. And I don't doubt that by the time we parted my new friend had laid to rest some of the common misconceptions he had picked up about just who Mennonites really are.

What I didn't have time to tell him was that I hadn't always been a Mennonite—nor why I had become one. That story would have taken more than an afternoon to tell. But it is a story worth telling—a story full of faith and family, of searching and of belonging. And it is a story about how God loves all of His children, regardless of how the branches connect on their family tree.

I offer that story now to you.

INTRODUCTION

WHY WRITE A BOOK LIKE THIS? To give insiders a glimpse into what it is like to come into their circles, that their understanding and openness might grow; to give outsiders a peek into what it is like to become plain, that they might be emboldened to join the fellowship too; to give both groups a vision of the God who is over all, that together we might overcome prejudice and fear to discover that we are really, after all, one-siders.

. . . . . .

Though the names of some of the people and places have been changed, and a few events have been blended to make the story flow, the events in this book are true to the best recollection of the author.

1

ON THE RIGHT TRACK

IT WAS FRIDAY NIGHT and that meant pizza. It was one of the things that tied all of us together—that and the Buffalo Bills. No matter which side of town you lived on, you could count on your dad bringing home a large pizza or two after work every Friday. Joe and I practically grew up on the stuff, and we knew where to get *real* pizza—the kind with imported pepperoni and whole-milk mozzarella from the Italian cheese plant on the West Side.

This particular Friday was a little different though. Joe pulled into our narrow driveway with two steaming pizzas on the back seat of the station wagon and our two-year-old son strapped into the car seat beside him. Colin was still too young to say so in words, but you could tell by the way his little booted feet kicked up and down that he was thoroughly delighted that this time his daddy had taken him along to pick up supper.

When Joe carried Colin into the house and set him just inside the door, the toddler nonchalantly held out his arms, clearly indicating that he expected his dad to help him get out of his snowsuit. Joe unwrapped the child who, now liberated, ran off to find his mom and older sister. Joe headed back outside to bring in the pizza.

He opened the front passenger door but the pizzas were not on the seat. He must have put them in the back. No, they were not there either. When he looked through the back window, he saw only an empty seat. The boxes were gone! In the time it had taken him to carry in and unwrap his son, maybe five minutes at most, someone had walked up his driveway—his driveway—opened his car door, and stolen his supper!

Joe scrutinized the neighboring porches, stared along the sidewalks, listened for a closing front door, but there was no sign of the thief.

"This is ridiculous!" Joe fumed over his bowl of boxed macaroni and cheese a half-hour later. "First someone steals Meghann's bike, then we find used needles on the curb, and now someone's got the nerve to steal pizza from the car when I'm practically on the front porch! They must have known I would be right out to get it! How could they be so bold?"

Joe was really angry—and troubled. He was worried for the children. He put a large gate across the driveway, but we still did not feel like they would be safe playing outside alone. The neighborhood was full of bullies and thieves. He had not forgotten that just a few months before, a drunken gunman had calmly walked into the corner pizzeria and shot the delivery boy because he wanted the money brought in from a single night of business. The delivery boy died, and now a sheet of bullet-proof glass separated the customers from the workers who had become almost a part of their families.

And those were just the physical dangers. How could we teach our little ones to follow God in a place that tolerated, even encouraged, violence and immorality like this? Few of our neighbors were practicing Christians, and even the ones who were allowed their children to do things we never wanted our children to do.

It was an impossible dream, though, to get out of the city. Nobody ever left. You were born here and you died here. It is just the way it was. Only the wealthy could afford to move, and we did not even have a savings account. Besides, Joe was a computer technician, and we could not imagine finding very many technical jobs in the countryside that surrounded the city of Buffalo. So we put up the gate and prayed.

During the long wait, God sent us two more sons. And even though we pulled Meghann out of school and began to home-school them all, the children were starting to show the strain of living in two worlds. The homemade soup and Bible memory verses they were fed at our house were countered with junk food and violent video games at their friends' homes. Even three-year-old Evan and little Nate were asking to play with toys from children's TV shows rather than with the trikes and Legos we had bought for them. And we didn't watch TV!

Joe and I begged God for relief for six years. We switched churches several times in a desperate search for other families—for even one that believed like we did. But it seemed that everywhere we went people spoke more righteously than they acted. Even youth groups and Sunday schools seemed like dangerous places for children.

Then one day, and with a bit of humor, God began to answer our prayers. It happened at the statewide homeschool convention we attended during our second year of homeschooling. We went there to find a seventh grade curriculum for Meghann and something that would do a better job of teaching six-year-old Colin how to read. We thought we might also like to get a few little workbooks for Evan who was almost three and very interested in his older siblings' schoolbooks. The convention featured a huge curriculum sale where dozens of vendors from around the country came to sell what were, in their opinions, the best books on the market.

Dizzy from walking up and down the countless rows of tables, trying to sort through all the choices we had to make, our attention was grabbed by several small groups of people in unusual, but not unattractive, clothing. They were called Mennonites. The men all looked like they were on their way to a meeting with their neatly trimmed hair and button-down shirts. And the women wore lovely dresses with an extra cape built right over the bodice for modesty. We figured the ladies all had long hair, but it was covered by some sort of cap or headscarf so it was hard to tell.

The most unusual thing about them, though, was not their clothing—it was their teenagers. I can still picture the trio walking past the tables, arm in arm, giggling like best friends do when they are talking about what they did over the weekend. At first I thought they were three teenagers, but then I noticed it was really a mom with two teenage daughters! I could not take my eyes off them.

They talked and smiled and related to one another as if they actually enjoyed being with one another. It was so different from the haughty disdain and downright rebellion I was used to seeing in young people. The smaller girl, her head scarf merrily swinging as she continued with the conversation, looked up into her mom's eyes and said something that made the older woman chuckle. Then the taller girl noticed something on one of the tables they had just been about to pass, and they all turned to look at it together. Their conversation continued the entire time.

My own daughter, whom I had left at home, was only eleven, and when I looked at that radiant mother with her happy daughters, I glimpsed a vision of how it could be in the teen years. I wanted that vision to include Meg and me.

The Mennonite vendors were different too. Unlike most of the homeschooling companies, who jam-packed their tables with the goods they were selling for a profit, these folks were selling low priced books from nonprofit companies. They even piled a section of their tables with tracts that you could take for free. None of the other vendors did that. We could not help but wonder what motivated them. Why were they working if they made no money from their sales? Why did they dress like that? Why did their families seem so much happier than the families we knew?

Joe and I both were fascinated by the Mennonites, but we were embarrassed to admit this to each other. Why? We are not sure. But we think that fear was part of the reason—fear of change, of looking strange, of the possible repercussions. We were not normally shy about discussing things with each other, but the Mennonites seemed so different somehow that it was almost too shocking to admit that we found them attractive. I mean, they were all born into Mennonite homes, but we were born Catholic, and the gulf between our two worlds seemed impossibly wide.

All of this might explain why Joe waited until I was in another part of the building to scoop up a batch of the most interesting looking material from one of the Mennonite vendor's "free" section and squirrel it away in his bookbag. It also explains why I waited until he was out of sight before I picked up some tracts for myself. I could hardly wait until he went to work on Monday so I could read them. But that would have to wait. Like Joe, I tucked my prize into an inner pocket of my bag and turned my attention back to finding some good curricula for the upcoming school year.

As soon as Joe had pulled out of the driveway Monday morning and the children had finished saying their memory work and settled down with their schoolbooks, I hurried off to get my tracts. More than once either Meghann or Colin had to pull me from my reading to attend to some question they had about their lessons. But the long fast of my soul was ending, and I could not seem to take in the material quickly enough. I devoured each paragraph, relished each bite until, finally sated, I turned my attention back to my children. I read about living in this world without being entrapped by it; practical ways to love my enemies; why television is harmful to the soul; and why it is good for women to dress modestly. And I found out how it was that the mother at the convention had won the hearts of her two girls. I was hooked! A few weeks later, after I had read and re-read the material many times and had cross referenced it with the Bible references given on just about every page, God arranged for Joe and me to have a little meeting. It happened like this. I was waiting for Joe to come home from work when I noticed what I thought was my pile of tracts laying on the dining room table. "Hmm? I don't remember leaving those there. I'd better hide them quickly before Joe gets home." As I opened the dresser drawer to put away my secret literature, I think I actually smiled when I found there was already a pile of tracts in the drawer. What I was holding must be a second set of tracts belonging to Joe!

I greeted Joe at the door with a set of tracts in each hand and a brief explanation of what I thought was going on. We could barely wait till supper was over so we could put the children to bed and talk alone. While I chuckle at the picture of us hiding literature from each other, I realize that in His wisdom God had given each of us the time we needed to wrestle with the big changes that were sure to follow if we acted upon the information we had been reading.

One of the first things we decided to do was to order our curriculum from Christian Light Publications (CLP), one of the Mennonite publishers who had printed and distributed the tracts we had been reading. Their workbooks had a great format for teaching in a multi-grade home, and the two older children really enjoyed them. But what I liked even better than the workbooks were the library books. I bought one of everything CLP sold, it seemed, and I could not read it all fast enough. I felt like I was finally finding some of the fellowship I had been hungering for, even if it was only in books. Real authors were speaking to me about real issues, and I loved the excitement they had about their Christian walk. I even bought a bunch of books about Anabaptist history and developed a unit study for the children. We spent that summer reading large chunks of history aloud each day and memorized the Sermon on the Mount as a companion passage.

The Bible verses came alive like they never had before when I read about Dirk Willem returning good for evil in *The Drummer's Wife*, or of Michael Sattler giving everything he had to gain the kingdom of God in *Pilgrim Aflame*.

We also decided that I should start wearing some sort of head covering. I had no clue how to make one of the pleated mesh caps I had seen on so many heads at the homeschooling convention, but I wanted something different than just a regular old work scarf. So I got some lacy white fabric, cut it into my best approximation of a head shape, and sewed it onto a large barrette. I already had long hair, but I had no idea how to "put it up," so I just braided it into a plain old ponytail and clipped the little covering onto the crown of my head.

It was really quite a small covering, now that I look back at it, and much fancier than my current ideas of modesty, but at the time it felt monstrous and glaring. I was sure the thing lit up my head like a neon sign that said to every passerby, "Look! Here is a strange one!" My extended family thought it was ridiculous and told me so with words like, "Hey, Becky! What's with the head gear?" and "What's that coffee filter you've got on your head for?" And they laughed.

The ladies at church also stared. One woman who used to wear a covering herself when she had belonged to a Brethren Church leaned over to me at choir practice and said in a conspiratorial voice, "You should talk to my husband. He can help free you from that." I didn't quite know how to blend my newly learned "returning good for evil" with an unashamed defense of my position, so I simply said, "But I don't want to be freed from it!"

"Hey Joe," I said hesitantly one evening. We were sitting on the couch watching the gently falling snow by the light of the street lamp outside. The children were in bed upstairs. It seemed like a good time to broach the subject. "You know, we're the only ones I know who are living like we do—except the Mennonites—

and it's kind of lonely for me. What would you think about me going down to one of the teacher training courses they hold at CLP? We've been using their schoolbooks for half a year now, and I really like them. Besides, I would get to stay with a Mennonite family for a week," I quickly added. "I would really like that. And I could see if the people are really like they say they are in all their books."

"Well, I wouldn't mind your going and you could use some time off," he answered. "But what if you really like it down there?" Anxiety was unmistakable in the way he asked the question.

"I don't know," I answered. "There's just something in me that still isn't satisfied. I want to know if it's all true. Do people really live this way all the time? And what are they like?" We had read so much about Mennonite life over the past few months that, although it was an exciting thought, it seemed almost unreal that there could really be whole groups of people that believed like we did and actually put their beliefs into practice. But if they did, I wanted to know what it was like.

"Yeah," he said not sarcastically, "I'd like to know too. But even if they do, what difference would that make to us? I mean, it's not like we could join them on Sundays. Virginia is awfully far away."

"I know. But it wouldn't hurt to just go and see what they're like."

"All right. You set up your reservations, and I'll arrange for your mom to watch the children when I'm at work," Joe finally said. "Who knows, I might even follow you down there," he added with that grin of his, and it was settled.

My week in "the Valley," as they called it, flew by. I could hardly catch my breath between the excitement of staying with a real, live Mennonite couple, touring the countryside, and studying for all my lessons. I was so happy. It is hard to explain how at ease I was. I felt like I had finally come home. It was not long before I knew that if Joe didn't want to move to Virginia, I was going to have to live the rest of my life with a profound feeling of loss and un-belonging.

Fortunately, Joe's and my soul are pretty tightly woven together, and he could tell as soon as I got home that I had left part of my heart in Virginia. He saw that I had developed a very real longing for a far away place and for a people he had only met in schoolbooks. Only a few months went past before he decided to journey south too. He wanted to experience for himself what it was that had so enamored me.

"Hello, Mr. Landes?" Joe said into the receiver. "I'm Joe McGurrin and my wife, Be...."

"Oh, Becky!" The voice on the phone broke in. "Why, she sure fit right in here. I told my wife to just watch and see if Becky doesn't come back to us within a year!"

Joe could hardly get in a word, and without much effort on his part, the whole family was soon invited to come down and visit the Landes's for a few days to "check out" the church and get to know the people.

The people at Bethany Mennonite Church, where the Landes's were members, were as anxious to meet us as we were to spend time with them. Before the visit was over, we had taken a flash tour of Christian Light's facility, gotten a job interview for Joe, attended a prayer meeting, toured a house for rent, and ate in the homes of ten different families. It was exhausting!

Of all that impressed us on this trip (and there was a lot), it was the Mennonite spirit that we found most attractive. The people seemed to be genuinely happy with their choices in life and radiated a joy that could only come from a peaceful, contented relationship with God. It was like we had stepped into one of the storybooks we had been reading, and we loved it.

On the drive back to Buffalo, all six of us were buzzing with excitement over what we had just experienced. None of us really wanted to go home very much. Where was home now anyway? It was confusing. As Joe and I talked candidly in the front seat about what choices were facing us now that we had been offered a possible job and a house to rent in Mennonite country along with the kind of church we had dreamed about for years, Meghann, then fourteen, said from the back seat, "I know those people back there are living the right way, but I can't go home and be the only one in my youth group who wears a covering. There's no way I could do that alone."

Joe gave me a look that said, "Do we need to discuss this any longer?" How could we even consider staying in Buffalo when one of our children had made such an honest confession. For her sake, for all of our sakes, we were going to have to move very soon.

The first thing Joe did when we got back to Buffalo was put in his resignation at the small college where he worked. Then he told me I had one week to sort through the house and get everything ready for a giant garage sale.

"A week? You've got to be kidding! How in the world?" I asked with no mild expression in my voice. "I couldn't possibly be ready that soon."

"You have to be," he answered tenderly but firmly. "I've put in my notice at work, and I only have two weeks left there now. They will be looking for me at CLP two weeks from today. I'm thinking we should sell all we can. We can buy new stuff in Virginia if we need it. Besides, the house we'll be renting is too tiny to hold everything we own. Then, when the sale is over, you'll have a full week to pack up what's left."

"A *full* week. What's so full about a week?" My dear husband seemed quite confident that I could do the impossible. I thought he had lost his mind!

But somehow we did it. In a fuzzy blur of nonstop activity, we sorted, displayed, and sold everything we possibly could. Joe was wise to encourage me to focus only on the sale that first week. The second week would be plenty of time to pack what remained, he said. One thing at a time. As Saturday drew to a close, I gathered everything from the sale tables that had not sold and packaged it up to take to charity. I counted the money in the cash box. We had made enough money from the sale to pay for a medium-sized moving van. Hallelujah!

The second week we had much less left to pack for the move, but it was still way too much to fit in the van. We were forced to abandon over half of our remaining possessions. So we packed only the bare essentials and a few treasured mementos. It is strange how you can gather up a houseful of useless possessions without really trying, and then you think you need them all. It was actually a relief to be forcibly freed from the chains of ownership—at least from a large portion of the goods that had been piling up over our lives and weighing us down. It was all quite exciting.

There was one thing, though, that dampened our excitement: the visitors. Oh, a few came to cheer us on, but those were mostly the distant acquaintances. The people we were really close to—family and dear friends—came to plead with us, to help us see reason, and to grieve. Many thought they were losing us to a cult. We felt helpless to comfort them. How could we explain the joy we felt at getting out of what, to them, seemed good and normal? How could we reassure them that we still did, and always would, love and treasure them? It was all so very hard.

When they left, we would turn back to our packing, and the excitement would return. It was a mixed and strange time. Through it all, though, we felt a confidence and a deep conviction that we were doing a very good thing. We looked crazy to them, but we were not. We were following God, going like Abraham into a new and strange future whose details were known only to God.

2
THROUGH THE LOOKING GLASS

"Oh, Joe, I just can't drive any longer!" I cried into the two-way radio I held in my hand beside the steering wheel. "I can't see a thing. Even your tail lights have disappeared, and I can't tell where the edge of the road is!"

"Listen," reassured Joe, "I'm going to slow the truck down to five miles per hour. You slow down to seven or eight and you should see me soon. Okay?"

"Uh huh."

"Here we go. I'm at about twenty miles per hour now, slowing to eighteen, fifteen, twelve, ten. Are you slowing too?"

"Uh huh."

"Good," whispered Joe. I'm at ten now, and you should be about there too. I'm going to slow to five so watch for me, then match my speed." He sounded so confident.

"I will… there! I see your lights! Oh, thank you, God!" I added only half audibly. Tears of mingled stress and relief dripped from my eyes as I gratefully steered the loaded station wagon in behind the moving van. The fog was so unbelievably thick in the mountains between Buffalo and Virginia. I was pretty sure we were going to reach heaven before we ever made it to our new church home. We had already been lost in the fog two or three hours, and my emotions had become quite feminine. I was sure I could not possibly go on. And yet, we could not pull over because, for all we knew, we were in the middle lane of the interstate; the road lines had completely disappeared. I could not, and yet I had to. It made no sense. Emotion was all I had left to keep me going—that and some strange kind of autopilot.

"You still there, Babe?" came Joe's reassuring voice over the radio again. "Hey! I think we're on some kind of off-ramp." Sure enough, Joe had calmly led us through zero visibility, hugging what he thought was the side of the road, until he found us safely tucked into a nice, out of the way corner of an invisible parking lot.

We waited there for a few more hours before the fog lifted enough for us to resume driving. When it was all over, our nine-hour trip had grown to sixteen hours, much of it through the most stressful conditions. Only God's unexplainable grace and protection could have kept me focused and Joe awake for such a difficult journey.

It was late Saturday evening when we finally pulled into the driveway of the house we had rented in the farming country near CLP. To our astonishment, the entire congregation of the Bethany Mennonite Church was waiting for us on the front lawn. In little more than an hour they unloaded the two vehicles that had taken us a full day to pack. They set up and made the beds, fed us a meal, left food in the fridge for the next day, and said their goodbyes. It was like something out of a children's storybook. We had emerged out of the fog to find ourselves in Wonderland. With sighs of relief, exhaustion, and pure amazement, we fell asleep in our own beds in a completely new world.

We woke the next morning to find that in the move we had somehow misplaced some very essential Sunday items, namely dress shoes and hair brushes. Had we sold them at the garage sale? The time to leave for church was fast approaching, and we were about to be very embarrassed to show up in sandals and sneakers with finger-combed hair on our first Sunday. Oh well, it was the best we could do. Perhaps we seemed strange to our new friends in so many other ways that they would think this was how we normally went to church. But it did make us extra nervous to know that we were not even going to be able to put on our best Sunday look.

On the short drive to church, I gave the children all sorts of instructions and warnings (and probably a few threats). We arrived at the tiny white building pretty close to starting time and were greeted with warm smiles by several of the people who had unloaded our truck the night before. It startled Joe to see the men greet one another with a kiss of charity.* He was glad to find out that only the members greeted one another this way. He was not quite ready for such an intimate greeting himself. It did not seem as odd, though, to see the women greet one another in a similar way. We had seen non Mennonite women do that before.

It was strange, too, how even the youngest children called the adults by their first names. Was that a lack of respect? Come to think of it, they all called each other by just their first names, even the preacher. There was no "Pastor" or "Reverend." Not even "Mr." preceded their names. I kind of liked that. These preachers were so approachable, so much a part of the people they ministered to, that addressing them in a friendly and familiar way seemed somehow appropriate.

Okay, I guess I could handle the first name addressing since it was not a lack of respect but a sign of intimate brotherhood. But there was something else about the children that cried out for an explanation: most of them were barefoot! This was not Somalia we had moved to; it was one of the fifty United States. Church was so special, so formal, that we could not understand how you could go to church without shoes. The children were all clean and their clothes looked new and pressed. So where were their shoes? (Now I was *sure* they would notice my boys' sneakers!)

*This is also called "the Holy Kiss" and is based on the following scriptures (Romans 16:16; 1 Corinthians 16:20; 2 Corinthians 13:12; I Thessalonians 5:26; 1 Peter 5:14).

I did not have long to ponder the question, for we were soon surrounded by friendly faces and led through an unadorned lobby into a small, uncarpeted meeting room that contained nothing but a few wooden pews, a podium on a 6 x 8 ft. platform, and a clock. There were no chandeliers, no plants, no organ, and no stained glass windows.

It was there in the meeting room that Joe and I were confronted with our first social dilemma. The Mennonite men split off with some of their children and began to find seats on the right side of the aisle. The women went the other way with the remaining children and soundlessly slid into the benches on the left side of the room. What were we going to do? We were quite unprepared for this conundrum, and there was no time to discuss it. Neither Joe nor I had ever heard of segregated seating in church. How would we manage our children? The two youngest had never been in an adult service of any kind. And we were homeschoolers besides. Anyone who has had experience with homeschoolers knows that we tend to be pretty attached to one another, and we do most things as a family. It was remarkable that we had even allowed the two youngest boys to be confined to the nursery at the last church we had attended. How could we split up now? Which of us should take the children? A man walked up to the front of the room with an open hymnal in his hand in a manner that implied he would like to begin the service. We needed to act soon.

While we stared at one another in discreet bewilderment, a group of young ladies with smiling faces gathered around Meghann and swept her along with them to a bench near the front where they all sat together.

"Why don't you take Evan and Colin," Joe whispered in my ear, "and I'll take Nathan." All three boys apparently have extraordinary hearing, for Joe had no sooner said this than they clutched varying places in the hem of my jumper in a way that clearly announced to everyone, "Don't even try to rip me away from her or I'll let out howls that would disturb a deaf prison guard." Social expediency won out, and I took the three boys with me.

I strategically separated the two younger boys, one on each side of me, and told Colin to keep an eye on Evan while I guarded Nathan. The inadequacy of this strategy soon became apparent. While Colin, at eight, had a pretty good understanding of what the warning look in my eyes meant, Nathan and Evan were too young to catch such a subtle hint. They had spent their few years of Sundays bouncing around in children's church or home worship, and they were about as active as you would expect little boys to be who were wearing sneakers.

Picture me on the ladies side of the room without the help of Joe or Meghann. Place all three nervous, sneaker-wearing boys on the bench beside me and the following scene will make a lot of sense. Three-year-old Nathan, who had spent 16 of the past 24 hours in a car seat with no scenery to look at but fog, thought the benches were a lovely place to loosen up. Hey, they did not have any seat belts! He just wiggled a bit at first. Then he shifted a little. And before I knew it, he was experimenting with his posture. (Did you know you could somersault on a pew?)

While Nate tumbled and I attempted to retrieve him with all the dignity I could fake, Evan got lonely. So he scooted over, cuddled up to the lady on the other end of the bench, and fell asleep on her shoulder. It was really kind of cute I suppose—until he started to snore. It was one of those delightful little five-year-old snores that everyone but a mother finds adorable. Colin, adding my chagrin to his own embarrassment, kept trying to wake up the little sleeper, but Evan thought his brother's nudges were just another part of his pleasant dream and slumbered on. To their great credit, the congregation proceeded through the entire service as though this was the sort of thing they witnessed every Sunday. Is that what they mean by *longsuffering*? After the service, we were invited by the Albert Martin family to a meal that we called lunch and they called dinner and by the Eldwin Campbell family to another meal in the evening that we called dinner and they called supper. You can imagine the confusion all around as we three families tried to communicate when and where we would be eating which meal. It was really quite funny, I suppose, but it was starting to seem like we had immigrated to a new country rather than just moved south a few states.

Albert and his wife Sarah operated a dairy farm. Oooh! That sounded idyllic. Visions of Old MacDonald ran through the children's minds as they thought about what it must be like to live on a farm. Lots of cows and ducks and lambs and geese and cats and pigs—well, you know the song. As it was, the Martins did have a lot of cows and a few ducks in the pond. They even had a pig. But that was for eating so they did not name him.

After a huge, delicious dinner (lunch), our hosts took us on a tour of the farm. We started out by the little pond. Really, it was not much more than a puddle to those of us who had grown up beside the Great Lakes, but it had ducks, so it was big enough. One particular duck had hatched out some ducklings, and for some farmish reason Sarah was raising the ducklings in a bucket with a warming lamp. They were so cute! The boys petted them very gently, great delight beaming across their sweet faces. But when Sarah held one out for Meghann to pet, the young lady recoiled with disgust. Or was it fear? Or disdain? Maybe it was a mix of the three, but our daughter had spent fourteen years in the city. She was raised during that over-cautious and thankfully brief period when babies' pacifiers were re-sterilized every time they fell on the floor, and she was not about to touch a wild duck! It is funny to think back on the incident, for she is now all grown up and is married to—you guessed it—a duck farmer.

We left the ducks and wandered along the house and hedgerows oohing and ahhing over the incredible variety of absolutely stunning flowers Sarah grew. She had them everywhere, it seemed.

And when the summer was over, rather than let the wind and ice get to them, she snipped off the flowers down at the bottom of their long stems and hung them all in the loft of the garage to dry. This gave her an abundance of dried flowers which she used to make bouquets, cards, and scrapbook pages in the winter. I thought it must be a lovely hobby to have.

When we left the drying loft and came back out into the driveway, we entered Albert's domain. He was the master of the herd, and his plot was dotted, not by bouquets and ducklings, but by large flat discs he called *cow pies*. They were all over the ground, but they were dried already so they didn't soil your shoes if you happened to step on one unawares. And, unbelievably, the Mennonite children went barefoot through the cow-pie fields too.

Albert was rather proud of his farm. It was neat and well run and his herd produced plenty of fine milk. He offered to let us try some.

"Oh, yeah!" the boys cried, entering fully into the farm spirit of the day.

After smelling our way past the pig, we ended up in the *parlor* which is not a place to sit and drink tea but a place from which the milk is extracted from cows. It is not the sort of place I ever imagined finding myself on a Sunday afternoon. But it was fascinating. Albert walked up to a tank, drew off some fresh milk into a mug and, to our chagrin, offered us a drink straight from the tank.

"Um, has this been sterilized?" Joe asked.

"Well, no," Albert answered, holding back the grin that was trying to escape around the corners of his mouth. "They'll do that at the plant."

"Oh." Now we were in a bind. We weren't talking about sterilizing pacifiers here, but about a raw product from a bacteria-laden animal. We were torn between our city scruples and the belief that one should always be willing to lay down one's life for one's friend. Albert had surely shown himself to be our friend.

How long did we hesitate. Ten seconds? Fifteen? I'm not sure, but eventually the spirit of brotherly love and martyrdom won the battle. That is why, against our better judgment and fears of scurvy, rickets, and the bubonic plague, a couple of us tasted some of the milk and found that it was really quite good. Yes, very tasty. But none of us asked for a second sip.

The tour of the dairy ended with a trip back into the farm-house where Sarah offered us some ice cream she had made from the same unsterilized milk. Every last one of us surrendered his city-scruples when we got a glimpse of that creamy, tempting treat. It was delicious! As we drove out of their lane, one of the boys remarked from the back seat, "Well, that ice cream was so good that I'm sure the milk can't be *too* bad for us."

We had been a few hours at the Martin's, and we hardly wanted to leave, but Eldwin and Vera Rose Campbell would be expecting us. Albert had given us a map to their house. We drove down the asphalt road as the map indicated until it disintegrated into a gravel lane. This lane turned quickly left as it descended a mild embankment and disappeared into a small river! Surely we had made a wrong turn. We checked the map. We were in the right place, and there, where the road hit the river, Albert had written, "slab." Apparently, that piece of concrete peeking up from the edge of the river was a slab of road used as a ford when the water was not running too high or too swiftly.

Joe got out of the car and carefully waded out onto the slab a bit. The water was slowly moving and only an inch or two deep. He thought we would have no trouble fording there. When someone mentions the term, fording a river, I picture horses, neck deep, their manes flowing wildly downstream as their terrified rider, barely visible above the foam, grips the animal for dear life. But how do you ford a river in a car?

Joe restarted the car and slowly inched into the water, pausing now and again to see if it felt like we were beginning to float on the wheels or be pushed off the slab into the deeper water downstream. We got to the other side without mishap and looked behind us to realize we had hardly even made a wake as we moved through the placid stream.

Eldwin and Vera Rose did not own a farm. They ran a printing company in town. That was a little more familiar sounding. They lived on a hill at the edge of the Valley. The tour of their place took us through a beautiful park-like lawn shaded by many mature trees and bordered by straight tiers of flowers. It was the perfect blend of formal and relaxed. And there was a rose garden, too, with many different types of roses that Vera Rose kept, simply because her mother liked them so much. Her mom was deaf, but that had not in any way diminished for her the enjoyment of a rose. So Vera Rose grew them for her.

Mother lived right there with the Campbells in the basement apartment with a lovely view of the grounds and the mountains beyond. The way they cared for her reminded me of the beautiful mother-child love I had first observed in the Mennonites at the homeschool convention. This time it was expressed in a willingness to care for someone's needs when life has put them in a vulnerable position, but it was the same love. Vera Rose's mom needed her daughter. And the daughter needed her mother. And Eldwin needed them and was needed too. And so they all lived together on the hill among the shady trees and fragrant flower gardens.

There was no sense of rush as we wandered among the gardens. But when we were done, Vera Rose served up "just a small something" on the deck that was every bit as delicious and filling as the dinner at the Martin's. Do these people always eat like this?" we wondered. How do they digest it all? We were used to just spaghetti and meatballs on Sunday afternoon and maybe some cookies or chips later in the evening. But these skinny little people ate like kings! While I remember being offered a lot of food, I really can't remember what any of it was, except for the milk and ice cream. I think that is because, as wonderful as both dinners were, Sunday was not really about food at all. It was about people and worship and relationships. Food was almost an afterthought, a lovely and precious afterthought somewhat like diamonds might be a mere afterthought on a golden crown. And the Mennonite people were willing to share both the diamonds and the crown with us.

When I think of the Campbells these many years later, my mind takes me back to that first Sunday evening when gentle conversation, a basement apartment, and a rose garden all blended together to say, "family and love—these are things that matter."

3

IN THE GARDEN

THE NEXT MORNING DAWNED with much hope and anticipation. Joe was going to work at CLP, and we all shared his excitement. Think of it! He was going to work at the same company that had printed the tracts and schoolbooks that had made such an impact in our lives. It seemed incredible. He was not sure what he would be doing, but he did not care if he became the official sweeper. God had rescued us, brought our children to a wholesome place, and given us a church family. It was almost too much to be real!

The pile of boxes in the living room, unfortunately, was real. The house we had rented was smaller than we had remembered, and even though we had sold or left more than half of our belongings behind, it was still going to be a tight squeeze. We were six homeschoolers in a tiny ranch house, and one of the three bedrooms was reserved as a storage room for the landlords. Where would I ever find room for books? Toys? Clothes? There was no way to fit it all on the main level, so we had decided to sleep in the basement. We figured that once the lights were out we could pretend we were in a real bedroom. Besides, there was a bathroom down there and space for two bedrooms. It was a bit damp and rather non-traditional, but it seemed like the best way to use the building. That left us one small bedroom upstairs to use as a toy room and another to use as a combination den/school room. Add to that a small eat-in kitchen, a living room, and a bathroom and that was the end of the floor space.

The church folks had set up all of our larger items and even unpacked my kitchenware and put it in the most logical seeming places, but the living room was still piled high with boxes full of books, toys, computer parts, art and science supplies, clothes, outdoor gear (and maybe even church shoes and a hairbrush). I sat on the wing-backed chair after Joe left for work and wondered which box to open first. That is when the phone rang.

"Hello, Becky? This is Dianne, the pastor's wife." She did not have to tell me. She had one of the sweet voices—I recognized it right away. "I was wondering if you would like to have a garden this year. It's already the second half of May, but I don't think it's too late to get in a few plants. Many things do well with a shortened season."

Shortened season? I thought, why, back in Buffalo the snow mountains are still melting in the grocery store parking lots and backyards are too soggy to mow. What is late about planting in May? Besides, I was so delighted at the prospect of ignoring my pile of boxes that I did not care whether it was late, early, or just on time.

"I'd love a garden," I told her with real enthusiasm in my voice as memories of Vera Rose's rose garden and tiers of border flowers came to mind. "Of course, you'll have to teach me how to tend it all," I told her, "because I don't know much about gardening. But I'd love to have a few plants around."

"Wonderful!" she answered, and I could hear the smile in her voice. Dianne is one of those people who is forever serving others. Even when it tires her (which is not very often), she still beams at the thought of helping. "I'll be over in a bit with a few things."

This is one of those points in our Mennonite journey where a translator would have been most appreciated. Dianne is a card-carrying farmer's wife, and when she says *garden*, she does not mean a few rows of impatiens with maybe a tomato plant or two.

She means a produce patch.

I did not realize this though until she pulled into my yard accompanied by a tractor. Not a rototiller—a tractor. I tried to picture how one could use such a wide machine to make the delicate little strips I had seen at Vera Rose's, but I was the city girl and knew that I was totally dependent on others when it came to things agricultural.

Elizabeth Ann, another lady from church, showed up about the same time Dianne did. They conferred briefly about the project and came to some quick decisions. Elizabeth Ann then ran into town to pick up some seeds and a few miniature plants that had been started in greenhouses the previous winter. Thinking back on it, I don't remember ever paying for the plants. Perhaps I forgot in the whir of the project, but I think it more likely that neither of the ladies would tell me how much they had spent.

Dianne told us that we needed to first remove the standing weeds from the old garden patch.

"Where is that?" I asked. She pointed to a section of ground that was bigger than my entire backyard in Buffalo! The ground was heavily overgrown, and it was quite a chore to pull up the long entrenched weeds. The boys pitched in, and within an hour or so, we had the majority of the foliage removed and had *pitched it over the fence*. (I later learned that pitching something over the fence is what you do to biodegradable garbage. You may only pitch it thus if you also happen to own the land on the other side of the fence. It is an activity we would never have engaged in back in Buffalo!)

"I think this will do," Dianne announced when the last of the weedy stems were removed. "Now we'll just turn this ground over a few times and make it real nice for gardening." With this, she daintily climbed up onto the high seat of the tractor and began to plow up the ground.

She did not get very far, though. Apparently, the ground was so infiltrated with the tangle of weedy roots that still remained that the blade behind the tractor could not dig down very deep. It just bounced on top of the ground like a child's pull-toy that has fallen over on its side.

"What if I would ride on top of the blades?" asked Elizabeth Ann encouragingly. "Do you think my weight would be enough to make a difference?"

"We can try," answered Dianne. "It couldn't hurt." With permission granted, Elizabeth Ann hopped up on top of the plow attachment to act as a giant plow-weight.

Elizabeth Ann is a rather tiny woman, but her weight was enough to do the trick. In utter astonishment I watched as the two ladies in beautiful dresses drove around my yard, one gracefully perched atop the plow as she was pulled behind the tractor driven by her friend.

It took only a couple of hours for the driver and her plow-weight to plant rows and rows of vegetables: corn, squash, cantaloupe, onions, potatoes, green beans (lots of these), tomatoes, lettuce, cabbage, turnips (did I miss anything?). The plot looked as big as a small farm to me, but they said it was *just a small garden*. And there wasn't a flower in it. Who ever heard of a garden without flowers? Where were the tiers of impatiens? The several types of roses? Come to think of it, this so-called garden looked like nothing but a bunch of sandy, soily rows with an occasional tomato spindle here and there.

"Oh just wait and see!" the two women assured me. "With this warm weather and rain we've been having it won't be long at all before you'll see lots of beautiful little sprouts."

Okay, who was I to say?

When Joe came home from work that afternoon, he looked at the garden, picked up his jaw, and incredulously asked, "Becky, what did you do to the lawn?"

"It's a garden," I answered. "The church ladies put it in. Don't you think it's a good idea?" When he didn't answer, I tried to reassure him. "I know it doesn't look very impressive yet—it's just a baby garden," I told him with a wink. And then I recounted the incredible happenings of my first workday in *Mennoniteland*, as we called it then. He had trouble comprehending how two little women and a tractor could accomplish such a large construction project in just a single day. But there sat the dirt patch—evidence that my story was true.

Later that night as I lay pondering on my pillow in the pretend bedroom, I thought how that garden was a lot like me. I, too, had been nothing but sandy, soily rows once upon a time. If you had looked at me when I was a child, you would have seen only a barren, dirt-covered soul. A worldly child you might have said. And you might have predicted that I would never produce much more than thorny, inedible weeds. You might even have thought that my ungodly heritage was so deeply rooted that I was practically unplowable. You would have been wrong.

In those earliest years, before anyone could see even the hope of a flowering plant, God was sowing the tiniest seeds in my soul and patiently waiting for their germination. You see, during those hidden years, my parents loved me.

Neither my mom nor my dad had been raised in religious homes, but they wanted things to be different for their children. That is why, as soon as we were old enough to walk that far, they made us go to church.

Every Sunday I hiked through the neighborhood and across the field with my brother and two sisters to attend both Mass and Religion School at the nearest Catholic church. We started out with every intention of arriving at the service on time, but then we would notice some temptingly shaped stone that was just begging to be kicked. If the stone was round enough, it would take the assault without much rebellion and roll in a nice straight path from one block of the sidewalk to the next, and the next, and the next, where it would calmly sit and wait for us to catch up so we could kick it again. If it was a perfect stone, it might allow itself to be kicked all the way to church without ever bouncing off the sidewalk.

If we could not find a good stone, we would look for discarded bubble gum wrappers that had gotten themselves lodged in the corners where the curbs met the street. Some of these wrappers had offers on them for free toys. One year I collected enough wrappers to order five purple velvet cow figurines—one for every member of my family. That is the only Christmas I can remember having gotten "store presents" for everyone. I felt so accomplished. It had taken a lot of curb looking and wrapper washing.

The hike was even more fun in the winter when the stones and wrappers were buried by the mounds of plowed-up snow along the edge of every street (this was Buffalo, after all). Then we got to climb high atop the snow-hills and scout ahead for the slight glare that betrayed the presence of a frozen puddle. The first one reaching the puddle looked briefly at its almost invisible black ice and then lightly stepped onto its surface, all the while listening for the delightful crackling sound it made when the pressure got great enough. The crackling, of course, crushed the puddle under foot, so the next person along would have to trek off in search of another one.

After about half an hour, if we had not dawdled too much, we passed under the expressway bridge where the purple-blue chicory grew in the summer along the cement wall. Then we turned the corner and saw the church sitting proudly in the middle of the big black parking lot. St. Patrick's Catholic Church was kind of odd looking. It was really just one flat story on top of another, and it did not have a pointed roof or steeple like most churches had. That is because the lower floor, which was used as the worship area (the part we called *church*), was topped by another level of rooms that was used for a school.

Some children of wealthier families got to go to school there all week long. That must have been wonderful, I thought. I went to the public school most of the week and only got to attend the Religion School on Sunday and on Monday afternoons after public school let out.

When I asked my parents if I could attend the St. Patrick's school all week, they sadly told me, "It costs too much. At least you get to go on Mondays." My mom especially cheered me up this way. She did not use words like *blessed*, but she taught me the concept of being thankful for what I had rather than pouting about the things I did not have. She hung a sign on the fridge that read, *Quitcherbellyachin!* She said a lot in that single word and I took it to heart. Thanks, Mom.

The sanctuary, as the room in which we worshiped was called, was as oddly shaped as was the outside of the building. Having rooms above it necessarily meant that it had a rather low, flat ceiling, and this was supported by several very functional looking pillars. Or at least that is how it would seem to someone who was visiting for the first time. To me, though, it was like the vestibule of heaven. When I walked through the front doors, I felt like I had entered a holy place where God was waiting for me. Even the tiles on the linoleum floor were special because they were in God's room.

There was no running or loud talking in God's room. It was too special for that. Regardless of how spirited we had been on the walk to church, once we were inside we fell instantly into reverence. We blessed ourselves with a dip in the holy water and a sign of the cross, genuflected at the end of our favorite pew, then sat down quietly until the Mass began.

The service had switched from Latin to English when I was a baby, so all my memories of prayers, songs, and Bible readings were in my own simple language. When I did not understand something—as is the case with children in any denomination—I knew right where to look, the windows. They were beautiful! The stained glass pictures told, in enchanting colors, the Bible stories I heard each week. I studied them intently and dreamed about their stories. Was there really a sower who sowed those seeds long ago? What did Jesus really look like? How did He make such big waves calm down? Did it hurt really bad when He hung there on the cross?

Then the voice of the reader would bring me back to my surroundings just in time to hear the Bible stories for the week. We almost always heard one reading from the Old Testament or an Epistle, one Psalm, and a story from one of the four Gospels. Those were the best! The Gospel stories were the ones about Jesus, and I could not get enough of them. I think that is one of my fondest memories from childhood and one of the things about the Catholic Church for which I thank God. It was their faithfulness in reading the gospel stories each week that introduced me to Jesus and taught me so much about Him.

Since my folks expected all four of their children to both "make" our first communion (around ages 7-9) and be confirmed (age 13-15), we had to attend the instruction classes which were held after Mass every Sunday. These classes were very interesting, and, though school-like, they were taught at our level in a more relaxed way than were the classes we took at public school. We studied all sorts of things about the Bible and the church and especially about Jesus and how He died to save us from sin and hell. I got to begin these classes when I was a first grader. It was a really exciting time for me.

One day the visiting teacher, who was a young priest in my parish, came in to tell us all about sin, repentance, and personal prayer. I was fascinated! I had never heard that you could pray to God outside of the formal group prayers we prayed at Mass. I was full of questions, and the priest patiently and very kindly answered them all. When I told him that I had never prayed to God alone before, he suggested that I start right away that night, and he gave me some practical tips on how to go about it.

I could hardly wait until bedtime. I wanted to be all alone when I had my first talk with God. I do not remember all of what we said to each other that night, but I do remember that as I told God how sorry I was to have done bad things and how much I wished to be one of His children for the rest of my life, my heart became filled with an overwhelming love and passion for my heavenly Father that has never gone away. It would be several years before I would learn all about what it means to renounce sin and be born again and other essential doctrines of the faith, but it was that night, when I was seven years old that I first began my personal relationship with the living God.

Ever after, when I heard the parable of the seeds on the good soil, my heart swelled with joy that God had made good soil in me, and I often prayed that He would make the plants that grew from my soil be the kind that yielded a hundredfold.

Maybe this is one of the reasons I like gardens so much. I love to take slow strolls around arboretums and cottage gardens and even through the forest, meditating on God and His handiwork and what He has done for my soul.

I am no longer just a sandy, soily patch; I'm a real, plant-filled garden, and it is God who has done all the plowing, planting, watering, and weeding. Best of all, He has breathed His own life into me and made me abundantly alive.

My thoughts were brought back to the present as I recalled the garden Dianne and Elizabeth Ann had planted for me. Would it really be productive? Or would it all wither under my untrained hands?

A few weeks later, when the little green shoots finally started to poke their way through the soil of my new tractor-garden, I did not have a clue which were good plants and which were weeds. How can you tell them apart? They all look the same—green with leaves. I phoned up Elizabeth Ann who came right over to give me a lesson on vegetables and weeds, how to tell them apart, and what to do with each. I think I must have learned something because that garden produced a hundred-fold and then some. I ended up with more vegetables than I cared to deal with.

"Oooh!" said my new sisters with unmasked glee. "The Lord has blessed you!" They followed very closely with, "Will you be needing any canning jars or freezer boxes?"

"For what," I asked? I did not want to face the fact that I had unwittingly become a vegetable putter-upper. Each batch of vegetables with which I had been blessed required great amounts of weeding, bug squishing, picking, peeling, snapping, shelling, blanching, and finally freezing in boxes or packing in jars to be boiled. It was all a rather messy affair and one that was, I soon decided, hardly worth the trouble, especially when I could buy three cans of corn on sale for a dollar! It was far easier and cheaper to just buy food and save my time to do something else. Not that Joe does not enjoy a bit of summer hobby-gardening most years. I salivate just thinking about those incredibly juice-packed, sweet tomatoes he brings to the table every August. But for myself, I still cannot tell the difference between a plant and a weed. I do not mind, though, as long as God still produces good fruit in me of one kind or another.

4

FROM THE INSIDE OUT

N o one called on Tuesday, so I had no excuse not to delve into the mass of boxes in the living room. It was not that I was unwilling to unpack them. I really did not have a place to put all the stuff. I phoned Joe at lunchtime and asked him if there was any way he could get me some shelves to set up in the schoolroom. At least then the books would be accessible, and I really needed to get at them if I was going to teach the children.

But when he came home that night, he brought no shelves. Instead, he said, "Becky, pack our bags. We're leaving on Thursday."

"WHAT!" I hate to admit that my reaction was this strong, but it really was. "We've just moved 500 miles from home, to land on some planet whose name I can't even pronounce, and just when I'm starting to make a bit of headway on the boxes, you want us to move?"

"Oh, no. I'm sorry, Babe, I wasn't clear. We're not moving, we're going on tour."

"Pardon me?"

"Well, John Hartzler, the manager at CLP, called me in today to tell me that CLP is taking a bus on a promotional tour for a few days and he wants us to go along."

"*Us?*" I asked with unmistakable sarcasm. "What do you mean, us? I don't work at CLP. So what would I do? And the children certainly don't work there."

"Well, it's something about families and all. I don't fully understand it, but it wasn't exactly a request. I mean, he asked it like a question, but I don't think he expects me to say no."

The pleading in his voice and eyes was unmistakable. This was important to Joe; I could tell. But, oh, four days on a bus with strangers from Joe's work and me all the time trying to keep the children from doing something painfully embarrassing. I don't do strangers very well. I certainly would not like to live with them on a bus!

"Well, where would we all sleep?" I asked as a clincher, sure that I had found a loophole to this crazy scheme.

"In homes along the way."

"Uh, what exactly are *homes along the way?*" It was getting more dreadful by the minute. At least the CLPers were local strangers whom I planned to meet slowly as the weeks went by, but *homes along the way?*

The stress and change and emotion from the last three weeks finally overran my sanity and streamed down my face in an unchecked flow. There was no way I could imagine doing what Joe asked. I felt like running far away and hiding until I could shake off this nightmare. Joe gently gathered me in his arms, all understanding and sympathy and let me have my cry. He is really good at that. He knows just how tight to hug and how long to remain silent.

And that is how, less than a week after I had packed my bags in Buffalo, I was packing them again to go on a tour somewhere with some people I did not know to do a job I knew nothing about.

All trip anxiety aside, this project highlighted the importance of finding the missing church shoes and hairbrush. As it turns out, I never did find those few lost items, and I can't image where they got to. Joe simply stopped at Walmart the next day on his way home from work and bought a few replacements. I think he even had to buy a suitcase or two at the thrift store; we had sold ours at the garage sale, figuring that we wouldn't be needing them for a while. How little we know what a day may bring!

The bus was one of those big touring buses that store luggage in a huge compartment below the seats. There was even a place to hang dresses in the rear of the bus, but by the time I got there the rack was full, so I folded up Meghann's and my carefully ironed garments and stuck them in a plastic grocery bag. They did not travel very well that way and only added to the feeling that I was really going to be out of my element for a few days. It was going to have to be God and me I thought. How else would I make it through the strange waters when Joe was off on his assigned duties?

Much of the trip blends together in my memory. People who have since become good friends were then strangers. I do not even remember which of them were along on the trip. I do remember though that they were all very kind. It did not matter what their age was. They were much like the people at Bethany that we so quickly had grown to love.

The afternoon of the first day we arrived at a large retreat center where the staff quickly set up a curriculum and book display as a few of the men rehearsed the presentations they would be giving that evening. There was plenty of time to gather in the large ladies' lounge to freshen up before the crowd arrived, and Meghann once again found herself swooped up by the friendly young ladies. Perhaps they sensed how lost she felt among the strange culture and how much she longed for home.

As I passed by them on my search for an iron to press a little dignity into our very wrinkled dresses, I saw the girls teaching Meg how to twist her hair in a way that made it easy for her to tuck it up into a bun beneath the mesh head-covering one of them had given her. I have never quite mastered that twisting technique, but she picked it up right away. Putting up her hair has been easy for her ever since.

The boys were really darling, too. I think the younger ones were too overwhelmed by the newness of everything to do much more than stick close to me. And Colin cheerfully pitched in when one of the staff invited him to help her set up and stock a portable bookrack.

The first speaker that night was a very Amish-looking man with a fluffy auburn beard and dark suspenders over his crisp, white shirt. I was fascinated by his story. He and his wife were very much like Joe and me. They, too, had grown up in non-Mennonite homes and had found themselves longing for people who shared their desire to live a down-to-earth, hands-on, city-on-a-hill style of Christianity. He was the computer guy at CLP and his wife taught their children at home just like I did. Wow! Up to this point, I had thought we were the only transplants in the bunch. It was exciting to listen to a man who had successfully and happily made the transition before us.

It was kind of God to let me hear our Amish-Mennonite friend early in the tour because not every Christian I met that weekend was so inspiring. At one of the places we stopped, a smiling, motherly woman invited the two younger boys to come with her into a children's area to play while the adults held another meeting. The boys were delighted by the invitation, all shyness having been driven away by the boredom of listening to old people talk about schoolbooks for several days.

I smiled inside when I saw my little fellows happily exiting the play area an hour later. And then came the dart.

"Oh, *you* must be the boys' mother," she said in a slithery sort of way. Why did she emphasize the word *you* that way? "I can tell you folks are from the *outside* (there was that slither again) because your boys kept humming tunes from cartoon movies."

Cartoon movies? We had gotten rid of our TV before Evan was even born! Of course, they heard the TV sometimes at their grandparents, but even then my mom only put Christian videos on for them. But that is beside the point. The woman's comments were like a slap from behind. I hadn't had time to duck.

Since I had fallen in love with God as a seven-year-old, I had been an *insider*. How had I gotten on the outside?

All of the happiness that had been growing in tiny spurts as the CLPers welcomed us into their loving circle was crushed by a single comment. I had already left behind my home, my heritage, and my family to follow God and now I had become twice-orphaned.

John Hartzler's wife, Ruby, who sat near me on the bus noticed my sudden change of mood. "Did something happen?" She asked later that day. "You seem sad all of a sudden."

Ruby's question was so sincerely asked it felt like my own sister had come to comfort me. I found myself pouring out my confidences to her without fear or reservation. She patiently listened to the whole story. She nodded with sympathetic, "Mmm-hmm's" at just the right places and said, "I see" when the mmm-hmm's got old.

And then, when my heart's pain had been spread out before her, Ruby soothingly said, "Well, Becky, I think that lady doesn't know you very well. Don't take her words to heart and don't hold it against her. She probably hasn't gotten to know you like I have."

"Like I have," she had said. Like she had. Did my compassionate listener, my companion on the bus, my new Mennonite friend, really feel like she had come to know me enough to love me? She surely acted like she did.

I awoke the next day pondering the rejection and acceptance I had experienced in such quick succession. Was I a Mennonite or an Outsider? Which did I want to be?

What really is a Mennonite, anyway? If it was like the kind woman who knew how to listen with compassion and who had a heart big enough to love a stranger like Jesus did, then, yes, I did want to be a Mennonite.

After we were all picked up from the various *homes along the way* in which we had been given a warm bed and a hot breakfast, John announced from the front of the bus that we would have a little time off this afternoon to spend as we liked. The bus would be dropping the women off at a shopping area in Lancaster County, Pennsylvania. We would have about an hour to shop while the men went off to do more manly things.

That sounded like fun. I like to shop as much as any woman if you take me to a really interesting store. How disappointed I was then to see the bus stop, not at a bookstore, nor a museum shop, nor a science supply outlet—but at a fabric store. *A fabric store!* What in the world was I supposed to look at in there? I was sure it contained nothing but cloth and buttons! You cannot do much with cloth and buttons except make clothes and who wants to do that? As the bus pulled away, I wondered where the men were going. Maybe I should have stuck with them.

I was amazed as we stepped through the unassuming front door to discover that the interior stretched back through several additions and alcoves to encompass a dizzying array of fabrics. There were polyesters and cottons and poly/cotton mixes; plaids and paisleys and the overwhelmingly abundant florals; there were baby patterns and wedding patterns and even specially printed pieces that could be quickly sewn up into pretty little pillows.

The younger ladies clapped their hands together with delight as they showed off each new treasure to their companions like so many toddlers at a birthday party. The older ladies were more refined. They merely skipped down the aisles in their quest to find as many good buys as they could in one short hour.

The holiday spirit was contagious, and I have to admit that I did look at a few pieces myself. I did not quite know what I was looking for, but it was fun all the same, especially when one of the others would come up to me and ask what I thought of the piece she so obviously found to be perfect. I always gave the correct answer, "It's lovely!"

This was part of being a Mennonite too. Doing things together. Sharing in one another's quests and delights and encouraging one another when a little boost was needed. It was like being with my family and girlfriends all at the same time. It felt good.

I am not sure how they did it—perhaps the bus was late — but all of the women finished their shopping well before the bus returned. Not willing to throw away a chance to continue shopping, we walked across the parking lot to an area that was thick with tourists. There were a few outdoor stands over there so we could look at things even as we watched for the bus.

One of the ladies knew of an ice cream stand that sold homemade ice cream. You did not have to ask me twice; I still remembered the treat Sarah Martin had served me just a few days before.

While I was enjoying my cone, something happened that helped me to make sense of the confusion that had slowly grown in my spirit over the past week and which had been brought to the surface by the thoughtless comments of the children's supervisor the day before.

We ladies were casually milling around with our various ice cream treats, sometimes talking, sometimes looking at souvenirs on a little kiosk beside the ice cream stand, sometimes just enjoying the warm, sunny air. I was sitting on a bench holding the bag of fabric I had somehow found myself buying (it was a pretty fabric after all and would make a lovely dress).

Across the walkway was a woman dressed in slacks and a pretty blouse, her husband occupied with the cheese vendor behind the table where they stood. The woman did not seem particularly interested in the cheese, though. She was intent on the horse that was hitched to a buggy and tied to a rail across the parking lot.

I understood her fascination. I had traveled in a lot of ways through the city where I grew up—cars, buses, subways, bikes— but I had never ridden in a horse-drawn buggy. It was like an idea from a history book, and it had a romantic appeal.

I was not at all surprised when the woman lifted the camera she carried on a strap slung over her shoulder and took a few shots of the scene. I would have done the same if I had my camera along. But I could probably get some pictures like that when I got home. After all, there are plenty of Mennonites in the Valley that still use horse-drawn buggies.

But then the photographer did an unexpected thing. She slowly walked toward me and hesitatingly asked if she could take my picture. Why would she want *my* picture, I wondered. I was merely eating an ice cream cone. What is so interesting about that? That is when it dawned on me that the woman with the camera was not interested in the cone—she was interested in me. She saw me as something somehow distinct from herself.

My world, which had been spinning for the last few days, came to an abrupt halt mid-spin. The world was now upside-down. I was no longer a tourist enjoying an ice cream cone on a warm day. I had become a tourist attraction.

At first I felt conspicuous and embarrassed. Here we go again—an outsider. But wait! Yesterday I had felt like an outsider because I was different from Mennonites. And now I was feeling like an outsider because I was different from a normal American tourist.

I felt surprisingly warmed at the realization. A stranger had drawn some assumptions about me merely because of the people I was with and the way I was dressed. She thought I was one of *them*. They thought so to. All that was left was for me to decide what I thought about the matter. To which group did I really belong? To which group did I want to belong?

The deep-down part of me that can think through confusing things came to the surface and knew just what my answer would be. I would choose to be one of *them*. I had always been an insider in God' eyes. But now I would make a conscious choice to be unmistakably identified as one of His people.

5

PLAIN AND SIMPLE

WHERE I GREW UP, *plain* was what you got when you ordered an ice cream cone without sprinkles or toast without jelly. It was unadorned—with no extras. And *simple* meant very easy, almost stupid. Anyone could do it because it was simple. Not so anymore. I have found out now that plain may have many attachments like pleats, ribbons, and homemade icing and simple is seldom easy to accomplish.

Such is the life of the *Plain* People. Sewing plain clothes, buying a plain car, or fixing good old plain food so that one can live the simple life is a lot of work. This I learned when I attempted to make a cape dress for myself. Up to that point I had been wearing store-bought blouses under long denim jumpers that I made myself. It had been a pretty typical outfit for a homeschooling mom—simple, modest and easy to make. But the ladies at Bethany—actually many of the Mennonites in the Valley—were wearing the same style of double-bodice cape dress I had seen at the homeschool convention in New York. If I was going to join their church, I would need to switch to cape dresses eventually. Why not do it right away?

My mom bought me a top-of-the-line sewing machine when she learned what I was planning. She figured I was going to need a jam-free model for all the sewing I would be doing. It was a really nice Bernina that promised to practically do the sewing for me.

I was beginning to understand the delight the CLP women had expressed during our trip to the fabric store a few weeks ago. If one is to sew one's own clothing, it is nice to have a supply of good fabric.

I pulled out the white/blue calico piece I had bought that day in Lancaster and laid it out on the carpet. Hmm, I was going to need a pattern. Where do Mennonite women get their patterns anyway? I called Dianne on the phone, and she told me they borrow from each other, and then modify until they develop a pattern that is just right. I folded the fabric back up into a nice, neat package and put it right back on the shelf.

Later that week the ladies at church discussed my dilemma. With innate perception, they scrutinized one another's arm length, studied each other's girth, analyzed one another's stature, and quickly determined who had a body that was shaped most like mine. Sister Look-alike promised to copy off her pattern and get it to me within a few days.

Normally, a woman would modify a new pattern to her exact measurements, so I compared the new pattern to the one I had been using for my jumpers. That ought to do the trick, I thought.

I pulled my pretty calico fabric back off the shelf, laid it on the carpet and, with a foreboding born of experience, began to cut.

The Bernina worked up to its name. But it could not do anything about the pattern I was working with. When I tried on the completed dress, I looked nothing like Sister Look-alike; I looked like a woman dressed in a white and blue Christmas tree. That is what happens when you cross a cape dress with a jumper. You get a Christmas tree.

Okay, so I am not very good at making dresses. I was sure to get better with practice, but I would need to find another fabric store before I could try to improve my skills. In the meantime, I turned my attention to Joe's need for a Mennonite style suit coat to wear on Sundays.

These are just like the suit coats you buy at JC Penny except the collar doesn't fold over to make lapels. Instead, the coat buttons all the way up to its little ridge of a plain collar. Plain suits were nice in that they allowed the men to look formal and dressed-up without requiring them to wear neckties—an expensive accessory many saw as needlessly showy and fashionable. To make a plain coat, one simply had to iron out the lapel folds, open up the neck seam, and insert a little rectangular collar made from some bits of fabric scavenged from the inner lining of the coat.

Most of the sisters at church had the good sense to hire a seamstress to do the conversion, but I was sure I could do the job myself. How hard could it be to make a little rectangular collar? Besides, it cost money to hire a seamstress, and I was not used to paying people to do work for me that I could do just as well myself.

I went to the thrift store, bought a jacket that fit Joe nicely, and quickly ripped off the old, lapel-style collar. Fifteen hours later, many of them with the stitch-ripper, I had produced a garment whose collar sprouted from the shoulder seams like the tail feathers of the main character in a Dr. Seuss book. Joe would never be able wear the thing in public.

My husband is sweet, though, and so selfless that he received the coat with humble and sincere gratitude and wore it to church. I was so embarrassed by the way he looked that, for the first time, I was actually grateful that I could sit far away on the ladies side. Not that it made any difference. Everyone knew very well who had made the sprouting collar; it was painfully obvious that it had not been the work of a seamstress.

The ladies all came up after church to offer their congratulations on my *effort*, and to praise the *noble* try I had made, and to remark on how clever it was of me, and to exclaim that it was the first time they had ever seen anyone put a plain collar on a tweed jacket. Then they told me about the book sold at CLP that would help me the next time I wanted to try converting a lapeled suit to one with a plain collar.

I asked Joe to bring me a copy of that book the very next day when he came home from work. And the day after that I went out to the thrift stores again, but this time I bought a charcoal-gray suit with a matching vest so I would have plenty of extra fabric to do the job right. Another ten dollars and another fifteen hours produced a coat that, though not stunning, had some degree of dignity. I told Joe he had to wear that same coat until he died because I was sure I would never make another like it. I had learned a valuable lesson: hiring a seamstress was as wise as buying cans of corn at the store. I was no more a tailor than I was a gardener. But maybe there were other plain things I could do well. How about laundry?

Not that you can launder a plain coat; it is not that kind of plain. Since they are really nothing more than just revamped store suits, plain suits need to be dry cleaned. It makes me sometimes wish we plain folk would adopt a style of men's formal wear that we could launder ourselves. But I have enough laundry to do without adding Joe's suit coats onto the pile, so I will not complain too loudly.

I kind of like doing laundry, though. I like the way I can transform a jumbled pile of dirty, wrinkled garments into neat stacks of clothing that just beg to be worn again. I like the sorting when I reach into the pockets to rescue the favored knife that escaped the child's notice as he flung the jeans onto the pile in his hurry to change into his next outfit. I like to wonder what Joe was doing that he was able to get ink onto the back of his shirt. I like the way the topmost patch peels off with each new day of wear—a testimony to the adventures of a little boy who does most things on his knees. And I like to pray for each family member as I see the history of their days etched and sketched into the creases and stains of their pleasantly used garments. Laundry is a happy job for me.

I think I owe this fondness for laundry to my mom. She often hung our bedding out on lines that she had strung from the house to the garage. I supposed she had no choice since it is a rare clothes dryer that can handle the bedding for a family of six. Whatever her reasons were, I remember the absolute delight it was for me to slip into bed in clean pajamas and bask in the delicious scent that emanated from my blankets on laundry day. On those nights I fairly sniffed myself to sleep.

That is the way it was in the city, anyway. But here in the Valley things were different. The area around CLP has been called the poultry capital of the world, and it has enough dairy thrown in to convince me that fresh country air is not all it is cracked up to be. Here, hanging out the wash has to be done according to the calendar. It all has to do with something the farmers around here call *spreading season*. Let me see if I can put this delicately.

Every so often, farmers collect all the cow droppings they can get a hold of and store them in a big tank until they turn into a nitrogen-rich, foul-smelling liquid. I am told that crops do really well when grown in the stuff. (See why I don't like to garden?) Anyway, at certain times in the year, the farmers fill tanker-trucks with as much of the nitro-goop as they can suck out of the pit and fling it across the countryside. They aim to get most of it on their fields, but there is always enough left floating on the breeze to douse your car, soil your bicycle, and perfume your hung-out laundry.

Church dresses hung out on a Saturday when your neighbor is spreading can be ruined for several washings. It is for this reason—and a few others—that many women have alternate clotheslines in their basements. And if you are like me, you also have an electric clothes dryer to use quite often at certain times of the year.

Between spreading seasons, when the children were younger and needed some chores to develop their character, I did not use the dryer a lot. Instead, I would send the boys outside with the wet loads of wash and expect them to hang it all in the neat way I had taught them. It was not a hard job, and it was good for them to get out in the fresh air before starting their schooling. It was funny to hear them discuss age-old launder's questions like, "Do you hang jeans by pinning them at the waist or flip them upside down and hang them by their ankles?" I have heard arguments for both sides, and I told the boys they were free to choose the orientation that pleased them most—as long as the clothes were dry and relatively unwrinkled when Meghann brought them in later in the afternoon.

I can still remember one Saturday when we did the wash and got it hung up really early and then turned our attention to other things. We got so busy we forgot the wash was out until well after it started to rain. I had not gotten a clothes dryer yet, and so I brought in just the church clothes and draped the dripping garments over the backs of the dining room chairs. They were so wet that I knew they would not be dry by morning when we needed them for church, so I set a fan to blow on them and added the heat from a hair dryer. The room filled up with more steam than a closed bathroom after a long, hot shower. And it smelled absolutely wonderful.

Then there was the time I sent the three youngest out with the clean wash, confident that they were well enough trained to hang it up by themselves. When they did not come in within a half hour though, I got suspicious and peeked out the window. There was the laundry on the ground beneath the lines with Evan sitting in the washbasket which had been fastened to the chassis of an old baby carriage. Colin was racing him around the yard like a charioteer. Nathan, the youngest, was dutifully trying to hang up some clothes, but since he could not reach the lines by himself, he was not getting much done.

It was hard to stop laughing long enough to look upset when I walked out to discipline the boys. They were having such fun that all I really wanted to do was join in the play. I went out the door looking somber enough, but I could not hold the pose. My stern demeanor erupted into giggles as I flung all three boys into the basket and wheeled them around the yard. We had a blast!

The boys liked the ride so much they used the contrived go-cart for many seasons. They christened it the Australian Summer Sled. I do not know where they got the *Australian* from.

"Hey, Evan," Colin said in the most nonchalant voice his little boy's mind could contrive. "Hop in here and let's go down the hill." It was weeks later and Mom was no longer in the yard to supervise the event.

Evan was a trusting little brother. He hopped on the buggy frame and even smiled as Colin gave him a push down the hill. The way both boys tell the story, the trip was exciting enough to convince Evan that he did not want to pursue a career as a professional racer. But Colin meant no harm—he tried the same run himself after Evan was done and declared it *sweet!*

Thankfully, the boys still let me use their commandeered sled on laundry days. It was a real handy way to transport the heavy loads of wet clothing out to the lines in the back yard.

Doing laundry among plain people naturally induced me to want to try a little down-home cooking. I had never much liked food preparation of any sort, but maybe I would like it better out here in the ambiance of mooing neighbors and flapping trousers.

I decided to start with breakfast. What could be simpler? No more cold cereal for my family, I thought, in a temporary period of insanity. We are going to be like the country folk around us who eat cholesterol-rich meals of bacon, eggs, sliced fruit, and biscuits fresh from the oven. The eggs, bacon, and fruit were pretty standard, and I knew how to fix them. But biscuits? The only biscuits I had ever made came out of little tubes in the dairy aisle.

I was told that, for maximum nutrition, I should grind the wheat fresh in the morning and mix it into the dough while it was still warm. Grind the wheat? Yes, grind it. We ordered a grain mill and secured a fifty pound bag of wheat from the local bulk-food store. Then we gathered a good supply of butter, baking powder, and a cute round biscuit cutter and looked forward to the next morning.

I got up extra early—this was going to take some time I figured—and started the mill. The machine was loud enough to wake the rest of the sleepers in the basement. How convenient.

While the flour was still warm, I cut it, along with a little baking powder and salt, into the butter. This is when I became convinced that homemade biscuits are anything but simple. The recipe said I was to cut the flour into the butter until it resembled fine crumbs. Well, I do not know what the writer was thinking, but I had fine crumbs of flour before I started cutting it into the butter. Now I just had greasy, floury lumps!

At some point I surrendered to the mess and rolled out the lumps onto the counter (surely they'll melt into the dough as they cook, right?). It was time for the cute little biscuit cutter. The ladies at church had told me that I should handle the dough as little as possible and roll it out as few times as possible or my biscuits would get tough. What they did not tell me was what to do with the lattice that remained after I had cut the rolled dough into circles, nor how to get the sticky, lumpy biscuit want-to-be's off the counter and onto the cookie sheet.

I scraped the prospective biscuits from the counter with a spatula and set them on the sheet. Then I cut the remaining, hole-filled lattice of dough with a scissors into odd-shaped chunks and placed them on the sheet as well and put it all into the oven together. At least I did not burn them.

The family is always very kind to me at the table, and they gratefully ate what I had made. But I knew the little hockey pucks were not really biscuits. They were something different—something full of fresh-ground nutrients and an extra heap of "I love you" —but they were not biscuits. Perhaps I could learn to make bread.

I knew what the smell of baking bread meant to a child. My mom had often baked it when I was little, and I remember how its enticing aroma would practically draw me through the door after school. Mom's bread was incredible!

Mom made most things from scratch. Cookies, jam, canned peaches, sausage. She even made gigantic batches of spaghetti sauce and canned it in quart jars so she could whip up a quick goulash and still have it be homemade.

You would think with an example like that I would have developed a talent in the kitchen. But it did not turn out that way. I sometimes think that my sisters, Luanne and Rhonda, must have inherited all of Mom's domestic genes because they both love trying new recipes and fixing for crowds. But it is sometimes a real struggle for me to even think of what to make for supper.

It seemed I was striking out pretty fast in the plain world. Other than laundry, I did not excel at home things. I was not a natural with a sewing machine. I was clumsy in the kitchen. I could not see well enough to keep my house free of the sorts of dust and grime that bother other people, and I had no knack for decorating.

Still, I wanted to make a nice home for Joe and the children, so I put a real effort into trying to find special things to make them happy. I thought I had found just the thing when I came across a simple way to make fresh strawberry jam.

Vera Rose had invited me to go strawberry picking with her and her daughter. That sounded like a very interesting way to spend a morning with the children. We went to one of those patches where you could eat berries as you pick, so I felt like I would be getting twice as much for my dollar.

The patch was very neat. Clean straw was spread between the rows of berry plants. You could crawl along an entire row on your hands and knees without getting dirty. This was going to be easy!

It was easy. So easy, in fact, that my enthusiastic boys had soon picked several more baskets of berries than we could possibly eat. Once you picked them, you had to buy them.

"Oh, that's not a problem at all," offered the proprietor when he overheard me explaining my predicament to Vera Rose and Meghann. "You just gotta git some of this here Clear Jel and make yerself some freezer jam!"

"What's freezer jam?" I asked him.

"Oh. It's good. It's how you make the jam without cookin' yer berries. Why, it's like eating fresh strawberries in the middle of winter."

That sounded good; we all liked strawberries. And the thought of preserving them without enzyme-destroying heat sounded especially appealing to the part of me that was still a chemist. I added the required amount of Clear Jel to my purchase and quickly jotted down the man's recipe.

The first few batches of jam were fun. And the recipe did make a really tasty topping. Fresh berries swimming in goopy syrup. Yum! But how much jam does one family need? We filled all my pint jars and had to run to the store for more. Guess what I gave as Christmas presents that year?

The extended family was amazed when they tasted their jars of strawberry jam. "*You* made this?" they exclaimed in astonishment.

With a grin that concealed more than it revealed, I humbly replied, "Aw, it was simple."

6

UNDERNEATH ARE THE EVERLASTING ARMS

"Hello," I said into the receiver. We had been in the Valley a couple of months already, but calls from back home still came in pretty often.

"Hi, Becky! This is Greer. How are you? It's so good to hear your voice."

"Yeah, yours too!" I said to my long-time friend. Greer had been my traveling companion when I had first come to CLP for teacher training, and up to this point, she was the only person from back home who could really picture my surroundings or understand why we had moved.

"Say, Rich and I were talking about visiting you. He can't get off from work for several months, but the kids and I could come later this week. Does it sound like a good idea?"

"Does it ever! You'd be a sight for sore eyes. Besides, you're welcome any time. I told you that before we left."

"Great! We'll get packing. See you Wednesday, sometime early evening, I hope."

"I can hardly wait!" I told her, and I meant it. Company from home! Oh, I had to call Joe and tell him. He would be so excited.

But before I could dial the number for CLP, the phone rang again.

"Hi, Beck. This is Rhonda." She did not have to tell me that. I would know her voice anywhere. "I was thinking of coming down with the kids to visit for a few days. Pat can't get off work, but he says it's fine if we want to go. You got room for us?"

"This is incredible!" I told her. "Greer just called to say she was coming with Matt and Keeley on Wednesday. If you come then too, we can make it a homecoming!"

My sister, Rhonda, and I had been chumming around since we were little. We were close to the same age, liked many of the same activities, and had many of the same friends. She was also the one person I had in my childhood years who shared my love for God. Not only did we go to Mass and religion school together, but we also talked about our beliefs. Sometimes I would even lean over from my top bunk before falling asleep so I could talk with her below and we could say our prayers together.

Somewhere in our early teen years, Rhonda had met a neighborhood friend, Lynn Kappel, who attended the large interdenominational House of Prayer in the next town. Mr. and Mrs. Kappel invited us to come along to the children's Thursday Night Club at church any time our parents would allow. We gladly went as often as we could.

Thursday Night Club was great! The leader always started with prayer, and then we split off into different age groups where we played games, visited, maybe made a small craft, and had a snack.

After an hour or so, we all gathered back in the gym for a short, young people's service. The youth pastor read and explained some passage in the Bible or discussed some important topic with us.

It was half sermon, half informal instructional time. The pastor's tone of voice and level of eye contact let us know when to listen quietly and when we were free to ask questions. He used words we never heard at St. Patrick's like devotions, repentance, and being born again. I soaked up his teachings like a sponge, and

I always wanted to know more. It was the highlight of my week.

"You cannot serve both God and mammon," the pastor said with pleading conviction as he had stared straight into my eyes one evening. "You must choose between God and things. You cannot love both. Which will you choose to love?"

His challenge shot straight into my soul. Which do I want to love? *Things* had never made me feel warm and loved the way God does. *Things* had never calmed my fears in the dark and scary nights. *Things* had not filled my soul with an aching longing to know and to be known. *Things* were nothing. I chose to love God.

Actually, I already loved Him so deeply that it was not hard to determine not to be enamored by material things. I remember asking God to help me—to even change me—so I would not be too attracted to things that would pull me away from Him. God answered my prayer. Throughout my growing-up years, when so many of my friends were pulled away by the glitter of fashion and peer acceptance, material things—mammon—did not look very attractive to me at all. They looked foolish.

The first real Bible I ever owned also came from the Thursday Night Club. They gave them freely to whoever asked for one. Up to that point, all of my Bible reading had been in a children's story Bible. Now I had the real thing— God's very own words!

The club teachers showed us how the Bible was organized and suggested reading plans to use in our devotional time. They gave us lists of key verses and encouraged us to memorize them. And they held us accountable. They wanted to hear us recite the verses when we returned each week.

Thursday Night Club at the House of Prayer was also the place where I was taught that if I really loved God, I must also turn away from sin. They explained it all in a way that was so easy to understand. And they showed me the actual Bible verses to prove that what they were saying was true.

Rhonda and I loved Thursday Night Club, and we were thrilled that our parents let us attend so often. They even let us go one year to the week-long summer camp sponsored by the children's club ministry. It was one glorious session of club that went on for days. I could have stayed there much longer!

We were so blessed. We had the Catholic church that our parents required us to attend every week, and we had the children's ministry that we loved so much. And we had each other. Mine was a happy childhood.

And now Rhonda had called to say she was coming for a visit. And she was bringing Katlin, Quinn, and Shayla too! I really must call Joe and then hurry off to tell the children.

One of the things Rhonda and Greer wanted to do during their stay was to visit Washington, DC. My house was only a two-hour drive away, and we could all fit in a single vehicle if Meghann stayed at home to watch the two youngest boys. She didn't mind at all she said. At fifteen, she had lost interest in school field trips. Colin planned to come along with us.

I had been to the Capital once before, so I had a vague idea of where the most popular sites were. Besides, we three were used to field trips. You get a few maps, pack a lunch, and off you go.

It was July 24, 1998, and the day dawned mild and clear. We left shortly after dawn—three moms and six very excited children in a red mini-van. Conversations and reminiscences circled nonstop as we made the short trip to DC. In just a couple of hours we had crossed the Potomac and were looking for a place to park.

"Oh, there's a spot. See? See? Right there!" yelled Keeley from the middle seat. She was right. There was a nice big spot right along the road, directly beside the Mall.

"This is perfect," remarked Greer. "We can start right over there at the Air and Space Museum."

"Yay!" came a chorus of assents. It was, after all, the site everyone wanted to visit most.

As we piled out of the van, I thought about how strange I looked compared to these old friends of mine. The last time we had been together we had all dressed in similar clothes.

But the feeling did not last too long. As soon as we realized that no one was staring at our odd combination of styles, we relaxed and forgot all about appearances. We were still just us, after all.

The children were amazed that they could touch a real moon rock, peek inside a genuine space capsule, and view historic planes suspended directly over their heads.

"Wow! Is that the real *Spirit of St. Louis,*" asked Colin as he pointed to the ceiling in unmasked awe. One of his favorite picture books was about Charles Lindbergh's famous non-stop flight to Paris, and he could hardly believe he was actually in the same room with the famous plane.

After the children had gotten their fill of space craft, science presentations, and hands-on exhibits, we hiked over to the National Archives to view the Magna Carta, Declaration of Independence, and Constitution of the United States. It was hard to believe we were looking at the actual manuscripts—not replicas. We were disappointed though with the preservative gas that hid some of the papers behind a greenish haze. Still, it was humbling to stand in the presence of this collection of world-changing documents.

As the afternoon hurried on, we decided that before we left the nation's Capital, we really ought to see the Capitol building itself.

It was too late to get in on one of the guided tours, but that was all right. We would enjoy just wandering around and seeing things at our own pace.

The United States Capitol is a magnificent building! Everywhere you look you are treated to granite pillars, bronze doors, and baas-reliefs that are carved right into the frames and lintels of the doorways. Looking up at the central dome left us speechless.

I am not sure how long we wandered around the building enjoying all this fabulous architecture, maybe an hour or so. The children were getting tired. It had been a long day, and we had a few hours to travel yet before we could rest back at my house. Besides, the road where we had parked allowed parking only until 4 p.m., so we figured we would all use the restrooms and then begin the long walk back to the van.

I cannot say exactly where everyone was at 3:30 because things got confused very fast, but it seems that Greer was in the restroom with her daughter, Rhonda had Greer's son, Matthew, and her own three children with her near the gift shop, and I was with Colin in the middle of a marble-lined foyer watching the security guard give subway information to a family near the metal detector.

As Colin studied the guard, a man with a drawn pistol ran in through the metal detector. The boom of his exploding gun mingled with the sound of the clanging detector alarm. It all echoed and magnified as it bounced off the marble walls. Chaos erupted. Children screamed. Mothers grabbed them and covered their mouths so they would not draw attention to themselves. Everyone who was able to, ran.

Rhonda made it safely out of the building with the four children she had beside her. Greer shoved Keeley under a marble bench that rested against the wall. I threw Colin down behind a thick pillar and shielded him there. It was the only shelter in the center of the gigantic lobby, and it was too late for us run—everything around us was open space.

"Oh, God! Oh, God!" We cried out as we sank down, trying to disappear into the floor as shots began to explode from behind us as well.

The bullets that were fired from both directions ricocheted off the stone walls, and our pillar seemed smaller and smaller with every shot.

"Wait!" I thought as our cries threatened to swell into panic. "If we are about to die, at least we will not die like cowards with bullets in the back of our heads. If they are going to shoot us, let us face them while they do it. God can do with us whatever He wants to."

"Colin," I commanded as I held his quivering body and whispered into his ear. "We've got to pray. Now!" And as we prayed for ourselves, then for the policemen defending us, then for the gunman we saw a few yards before us, a peace that passes all understanding flooded our minds and hearts and we were enveloped in a very real, touchable shadow of wings. Safety encircled us in its everlasting embrace as we stood up and watched the events transpire around—but not to—us. We were safe and we knew it.

Strange as it might sound, one of the reasons I felt so safe was because I was so conspicuous. It is not that I had time to think about deep theological questions between bullets, but somehow I believed that the same head covering that made me feel strange among my friends was, to the angels, just as conspicuous. To them it surely said, "There she is! The one over there by the pillar. She is the one we are here to protect."

It is not that I thought that God had not sent angels to help me all my life, but rather that this time I would be especially easy to spot. I was wearing a sign that proclaimed to the whole world that my Father was in charge of my life, and I knew He would honor that proclamation. At least that is how it felt in the whir of the few seconds I was aware of my thoughts.

Two people died in that horrific battle, and at least two were injured, but our loving Father, who saw the whole thing, protected our little group from harm despite the fact that we were, literally, in the line of fire. I say literally because when we revisited the site a few weeks later, a guard on duty showed us where a bullet had struck and nicked the very pillar that had been our shield.

It is difficult to describe the emotional fog that followed that awful day. Some call it post-traumatic stress disorder; I call it a need to make sense of the incomprehensible. It took a while until I was comfortable in stone buildings, and I still do not like metal detectors. My heart races when I hear a shotgun somewhere in the distance. And, in some ways I still try to understand what happened. But one thing I know for sure and understand very intimately: the God of the seven-year-old girl's prayers and the God of the Thursday Night Club and the God under whose wings we sheltered are all one. And it is this God who holds me in His arms.

"The eternal God is thy refuge and underneath are the everlasting arms" (Deuteronomy 33:27).

7
A WORD WELL SPOKEN

OON AFTER THE TIME I learned the verse about the need to reject mammon if I was going to serve God with my whole heart, soul, mind and strength, I came across a poster in the Catholic bookstore downtown. On the poster was the poem, *If Jesus Came to Your House*, by Lois Blanchard. I had saved up some allowance money, and since the poster was only about 75 cents, I bought it and hung it right beside my bed where I prayed each night. The poem reads like this:

If Jesus Came to Your House

If Jesus came to your house
  To spend a day or two,
If He came unexpectedly,
  I wonder what you'd do.

I know you'd give your nicest room
  To such an honored Guest,
And all the food you'd serve to Him
  Would be the very best;

And you would keep assuring Him
  You're glad to have Him there,
That serving Him in your own home
  Is joy beyond compare!

But when you saw Him coming,
 Would you meet Him at the door
With arms outstretched in welcome
 To your heavenly visitor?

Or would you have to change your clothes
 Before you let Him in,
And hide some magazines and put
 The Bible where they'd been?

Would you keep right on saying
 The things you always say?
Would life for you continue
 As it does from day to day?

Would you sing the songs you always sing
 And read the books you read,
And let Him know the things on which
 Your mind and spirit feed?

Would you take Jesus with you
 Everywhere you'd planned to go?
Or would you maybe change your plans
 For just a day or so?

Would you be glad to have Him meet
 Your very closest friends?
Or would you hope they'd stay away
 Until His visit ends?

Would you be glad to have Him stay
 Forever on and on,
Or would you sigh with great relief
 When He at last was gone?

It might be interesting to know
 The things that you would do,

> If Jesus came in person
> To spend some time with you.

—Public Domain

Blanchard's words inspired me to scrutinize my life, to analyze whether or not my individual choices and actions were pleasing to God. It was such a practical way to think about holiness. And it caused me to make some changes.

I took off my earrings and tossed all my jewelry into the charity box. I sorted through my closet and put the clothes I deemed *too fancy* into the same box. I considered the books on my shelf and discarded those I would be embarrassed to be seen with, and I started to hear what the words in the songs I listened to on the radio were really saying.

I could actually picture Jesus sitting by my side when the family was gathered in front of the TV. Sometimes, I was overwhelmed with the thought that, were Jesus physically there, I would be ashamed to have Him see what I was watching. At those times, I would slip off to my bedroom or the kitchen to find something else to do.

The radio was harder to give up. I loved music. It was something cheerful that I had in common with my friends, my siblings, even my grandmother, whom I fondly called Dee. I remember her taking me to a concert that featured a popular singer we both enjoyed. The concert was held in the hockey auditorium, and we were in the cheap seats—a mile above the ice, it seemed, in the orange section. The singer looked like a little figurine down in the recesses of the stadium; I couldn't even see his facial expressions. But I was with Dee—that was all that mattered.

Giving up the radio then, with its associated music, would mean giving up a precious thread that connected me to Dee. "Jesus," I said one night in the still calm of my bedroom where we met. "How can I do such a hard thing? It is too much!" Jesus did not answer; He just waited.

The struggle in my soul was intense. I knew and believed the mammon verse. I knew that God had said it, and it was true. But how could He want me to give up an activity that tied me to my grandmother?

Sometime during the long struggle, I joined the folk group at church. We led the singing at Mass and at occasional weddings and funerals. We sang about things that were holy—things that made me think about God and that led my spirit into a worshipful contemplation of Him.

Without my hardly noticing, the music on the radio became less and less attractive as my folk-group folder swelled, then bulged with worship songs. When the batteries in the radio wore out, I began to sing the church songs at home, on the long walk to school, and during my chores. I sang all day long. As a consequence, I worshiped all day long too.

I don't know when I noticed that my radio had worn out and my records had become dusty. Dee never said anything. We were just as close as ever. But eventually I became aware that my internal music-center had been transformed. God had quietly and patiently honored the request I had prayed at The House of Prayer—the request to change me if there was ever anything that dimmed my devotion to Him. Popular music had become mammon to me, and it was dulling the intimacy of my relationship with God so He fixed things. He simply changed my heart.

A changed heart needs new heroes. The television actors had to go, along with the singers and even the sports stars. Where could a young girl find godly heroes in a world like mine? I knew one place.

In the back bedroom of a small split-level home on the end of a dead end road lived a saint. She was Dee's sister, my great Aunt Katie.

Aunt Katie had a debilitating case of rheumatoid arthritis, and the bed to which she was confined rested in the home of her son,

Marty. She was in constant and severe pain, but I didn't realize this until someone told me many years after her death. The smile with which she always welcomed me into her room told me nothing but that she was the happiest of women and that she lived a privileged life.

"Why, it's Becky!" she would say when I entered the doorway. "So you've come back to see me again. How nice."

"Oh, yes, of course I came back!" I responded with an answering grin. "I couldn't wait to see you again."

As I walked up to Aunt Katie's bedside, I noticed the little statue she had on the table. It was of a peaceful looking man who had just a ring of hair. On his long, brown robe were perched several birds and squirrels. And there was a little rabbit by his feet. It was a statue of the unassuming preacher and teacher, St. Francis of Assisi, my aunt's favorite hero. She said the statue reminded her that God is kind to all of His fragile little creatures and we should be kind too.

Aunt Katie was just as kind as Francis had been. I never heard her utter a bad word about anyone. If a heated political debate arose among the guests gathered around her, she always diffused it with some kind comment about the person under fire. If she needed something like having her pillow readjusted, she would say something like, "Would you mind propping that up for me, dear? Ahhh, thank you." She was gentle and sweet and unassuming and kind.

When no one else was in the room, Aunt Katie quietly listened to my problems. Only after I was all done speaking would she begin to offer a few, tiny wise and soothing comments. The way she did it often convinced me that the bad news I had confided to her was really good news after all. Why hadn't I seen it that way before?

When I finally pulled myself out of Aunt Katie's room, I always had my faith restored. All was well with the world. At least from the way she was looking at things. God was still on the throne, Jesus loved me, I had a happy family. Why had I thought of complaining?

Aunt Katie is one of the people who taught me to be an optimist, to look on the bright side even when it hurts really bad. And she prayed. Come to think of it, she is the only adult relative I can remember ever praying personal prayers. This fact wasn't lost on me. Aunt Katie adored God and I wanted to be just like her when I grew up.

I also wanted to be like the nuns at church who got to focus on God all day long. I thought they had the best job description in the whole world, and I imagined that, when I grew up, I might even like to become a nun myself. Maybe I could be the one who arranged the altar cloths so nicely each week. Or the one who helped the confirmation class with their lessons. Or maybe I would go to a far-away country and be a medical missionary. A nun and a doctor at the same time—now that would be something!

But the years had flown by and I had not become a nun, nor a doctor, nor a bed-ridden optimist. I was a wife and mother who was simply trying to live my life according to the mammon verse, with Jesus as my only Master. The best thing I could do to live out that verse now I realized, other than to adore God myself, was to raise my children in such a way that they would adore Him too.

Thinking on all this caused me to wonder: will Meghann find an Aunt Katie to confide in among the Mennonites? Will the boys find God-focused heroes to look up to? Will the Mennonite people be the kind of saints that inspire little children to love God with their whole heart and soul and mind and strength? Joe and I thought so. That is one of the reasons we had moved here.

We were a bit confused and disappointed then when Elizabeth Ann and her husband, Raymond, invited us to a dinner party on their lawn one evening. They gave every appearance of loving God and His church deeply. Why then, we wondered, would they be asking us to go to a lawn party when the ministers had recommended that we avoid events like that?

Maybe they thought, like we did, that the ministers were making a strange request. Most of the other items in the church guidelines made obvious sense: avoid television to keep your thoughts pure, do not join the military so you could love your enemies, etc. Only this one guideline really confused us. What could possibly be wrong with celebrating a child's birthday outdoors or having some friends over to share an evening around the grill? What was so dangerous about a lawn party?

"Should we go?" I asked Joe. "I mean, what about the minister's guidelines?" He thought for a bit, then decided we should go anyway. Surely, we must have misunderstood what the ministers were referring to.

I was really uncomfortable the evening of the picnic. Elizabeth Ann spread a nice supper on the cloth-topped table under one of the trees on their lawn. The meal was so satisfying we decided to wait a while before we broke into the watermelon, so Elizabeth Ann put it back in the fridge.

Next, Raymond took us on a tour of his bird feeders. He and his wife loved birds. The bluebirds would land right next to Raymond to snatch up the fat, juicy grub he placed on the railing beside him. And the hummingbirds were so used to Elizabeth Ann that they would stay in formation at the sugary feeder even when she stood right beside them. The children were enthralled. But my conscience was not having fun. How could I enjoy a party that the church had asked us not to attend? And how could Raymond and Elizabeth Ann look so calm about the whole thing?

Later in the evening when Elizabeth Ann went into the house to fetch the cold watermelon and Raymond stepped in right behind her to receive a phone call, I took advantage of the opportunity and leaned over to quietly talk to my husband.

"Honey, I feel really uncomfortable about all this. Shouldn't we do something?"

"What would we do? I don't think it would be polite to ask Raymond about it at this point. Let's just wait the thing out."

He was right, I suppose, but it was really hard to relax and enjoy the gathering. I felt like a hypocrite.

The rest of the evening ran smoothly. Our hosts seemed to enjoy themselves, and the children relaxed in the freedom they had when a gathering is removed from a formal living room.

A week or so later, I saw something that made me feel ridiculous. As I drove home from the store, I passed a big marquee urging people to attend the annual fundraising carnival sponsored by a local civic group. "Rides, Games, Food," it read. "Come to the Ruritan Lawn Party!"

I felt like an absolute fool! Lawn parties were carnivals! No wonder the church thought we had better stay away from them. If we had only had the courage to question our hosts when they first invited us over, we could have avoided a very uncomfortable situation. I would try not to make that mistake a second time.

That is why, when Elizabeth Ann called me a few months later to tell me something in her sweet, southern drawl, I screwed up the tenacity to question her repeatedly until we both understood each other very well. The conversation went something like this.

"Becky, that reminds me of what Amy Carmichael said about the toad on the *hera.*"

"The toad on the what?" I asked.

"The hera."

"I don't think I heard you right, Elizabeth Ann. Did you say Hera?"

"Yes, that's right."

Knowing full well that my dear friend could not possibly be referring to the Greek goddess, Hera, I asked her, "What's a hera?"

"Well, it's what makes the furahs."

"Furahs?" We were not getting very far in this conversation. "What are furahs?"

"Fur-rahs," she said in her clearest diction. "You know the little channels in the dirt that you drop seeds into."

"Oh!" I laughed. "Did you mean furrows and harrows?"

"Yes," she replied triumphantly with marked relief in her voice. "Heras."

This conversation was followed not too many days later by another minor language mishap when we found ourselves at Albert and Sarah Martin's place again.

They were entertaining a small group of people for the evening, and we had pretty well polished off a tray of apple goodie and a pot or two of coffee when her son arrived home, walked into the kitchen, and asked with disappointment in his voice, "Is the coffee all?"

"All what?" Joe and I wondered. But as neither Sarah nor her son went to the coffeemaker to pour him a cup, we could not tell what he was asking about the coffee.

We peeked in our cups. Everything seemed fine. It was a nice, hearty brew and the milk was not curdled or anything.

Remembering my recent experiences with lawn parties and heras, I leaned over to one of the other guests and asked, "Is the coffee all what?"

"Oh," she giggled, "It's just all—you know—there is none left."

"Are you meaning it's all gone?" I asked, with a heavy emphasis on the gone.

"Yes, all, by itself, means the same as all gone."

"Well, beats me!" I thought. "Some words down here have different definitions, other words are pronounced funny, and complex verbs do not have to be all there."

I was going to have to set a new policy for myself; when in doubt, ask—or risk finding myself at a lawn party without any coffee.

8

A SOFT ANSWER

THE NEIGHBORHOOD SURROUNDING OUR rented home was densely populated, considering how far we were from town. It seemed almost as if someone had bought a narrow strip of farmland, had thrown down a gravel lane, and then squeezed as many houses along the lane as they could without turning the place into a mini suburb. At least they hadn't paved the lane. Then we would have had to deal with cut-through traffic as well as congestion. Still, it was a peaceful retreat compared to what we had left behind.

We only had neighbors on either side of us. There was nothing but a field behind the backyard and nothing but a pasture with some cows across the lane. We had stunning views of the sky, an occasional passing horse and buggy, and lots of time to just sit out on the porch and think about how good God was to us.

The boys were like prisoners suddenly released from the Bastille. They played football on the front lawn, rode their little bikes along the gravel lane, climbed the big pine trees beside the driveway, and did all the things they had been too confined to do in the city.

They drove toy tractors in the dirt, waded in their portable pool, braided long grass ropes, and picked fresh vegetables out of the garden whenever they wanted to. They even had a couple of dogs. Well, they were not really our dogs, but they roamed the neighborhood freely enough that the boys thought they belonged to them. They were loyal and playful animals, and they did not mind if you were in a bad mood. That is what I call a good friend. The boys adored them.

Wolf, who sometimes lived up to his name, came from a few houses down. He was big and black and very protective. It was comforting to feel that if any dangerous animal were to approach the boys, Wolf would drive it away—or eat it.

Chipper was the exact opposite. He was white and lazy and didn't bother to even scratch his own fleas. Chipper lived down at the end of the road.

Wolf and Chipper were usually great to have around. They entertained the boys and kept vermin away, and I rather enjoyed a few slobbery greetings myself now and then. But there was one thing about the canine duet that really bothered me. They loved trash.

They were especially fond of the kind that could be dug out of our trash cans and scattered all over the neighborhood. The pair seemed to make a game out of seeing which of them could spread the most items the farthest and the neighbors quickly tired of their sloppy games. I understood their point of view because I shared it.

You can imagine how incredulous I was then when Chipper's owner berated *me* for all the trash that was lying about. I could not understand why she came to me. I had put the trash into the cans. It seemed to me that since it was her dog who was one of the neighborhood litterbugs, I should, by rights, be upset with *her!*

And I did get upset. I seethed. I did not show it on the outside—not to her anyway—but the family could tell that I was not happy at all with the situation. Unvented anger built up in me, along with feelings of helplessness and indignation.

The only other time I could remember feeling like this was in junior high school. We had only a thirty minute lunch break. During that time we were expected to leave our English class at the end of the junior-high wing, hurry up to the second floor to dump our books in our lockers, rush down the hallways to the cafeteria in the high school, wait in line for our food, inhale it, clean up after ourselves, and make it up to shop class on the third floor of the high school building before the bell rang. It was nearly impossible to do all this in thirty minutes.

Most of us found relief from the stress of our rushed lunch break by commiserating together about the injustices of the system. And we grabbed snacks at our lockers between classes to make up for the food we did not have time to eat at lunch.

But there was one girl who did not blend in with the rest of us. Something kept her from getting to the cafeteria on time each day. Of course, there must always be someone who is last in line, but with most of us we shifted around enough that we took turns being first, last, or somewhere in the middle. Not this girl. She was always last.

The latecomer took her handicapped position well enough for a while, and everything worked out all right for the rest of us. But something changed about the middle of the school year. She began to leave her spot at the tail and creep her way forward along the wall beside the lunch line in hopes that someone would yield to her threatening glare and slightly pushy elbows and let her cut into the line. Those of us who were already cued up squeezed closer to the wall when we felt her encroaching. It was how mob justice worked. When we resisted, she just pushed all the harder until eventually the nicer ones of us in line gave in to her bullying and we would dejectedly watch her being served lunch before us. It was maddening!

One day I exploded. I do not know if I was tired or had just finally had enough, but as she pushed and pushed, my anger seethed and grew. I held my emotions in until, in one awful burst, I swung my fully extended arm around until my clenched fist impacted her chest with a breath-swallowing thud! In my anger, I had knocked the wind out of the poor girl who was always late for lunch. As she struggled to regain a breath, I coldly looked into her suffering eyes and told her that she was never to cut in line again. I was angry, I was violent, and I was covered in sin. My Father in heaven was not smiling at me, but I was so angry I did not care. I had driven out thoughts of His sweet presence with my desire to strike out. After I had calmed down, I was ashamed.

The girl never did cut in line again. She was afraid to even look up when I passed her in the halls. Anger does that. It destroys the striker and the stricken in a single blow, and the only victor is the enemy of our souls.

I have not hit anyone since then. I seldom even feel slightly angry with someone, but Chipper's owner aroused in me that same helpless, bullied feeling that had tormented me in the lunch line so many years before. I abhorred the anger I found still lurking in the deepest recesses of my now grown-up heart. I knew Jesus expected me to return good for evil, and I wanted to obey Him, but after months of my neighbor's haranguing, I found my patience thinning as my anger swelled beneath it. How could I endure, or better yet, put an end to this weekly trial?

Remembering that the gap between loving and striking is narrower than I had once supposed, I took heed of my own failure and sought counsel from Eldwin Campbell, who was then our bishop.

Eldwin suggested that in order to win this battle against myself, I was going to need to find a way to return good for evil. His advice sounded good but too abstract. I needed something more concrete.

"Why don't you imagine to yourself that you really are the one causing an offense every week, and then try to think of some appropriate way to make amends," he suggested.

"I see," I said, finally understanding. "In my neighbor's mind, at least, I am the irritant, so I need to think of a way to soothe the irritation she is feeling from me." Eldwin's advice seemed very good, so I began to pick up the scattered garbage as though I had littered the neighborhood myself.

This tactic resulted in a tidier looking neighborhood, and there was outward peace for a while, but my relationship with Chipper's owner did not really improve all that much.

"Bake her some cookies," Eldwin suggested. "You have only stopped the irritation. Now you need to go further and return good for the evil you have experienced. Give *real* love in return. That's part of what Jesus meant. It's we who have to go the extra mile. And remember to be gentle," he added like a soft echo from the Old Testament—"a soft answer turns away wrath" (Proverbs 15:1, NKJV).

I understood what the bishop was suggesting, but he was asking a lot. I had already picked up someone else's mess several times over, and she had never even thanked me. She still acted like I was to blame. And now I was supposed to do something extra? Bible verses are easy to read, but they can be mighty hard to live out sometimes.

Grr! I snarled as I mixed up a batch of chocolate brownies. They were my own favorites, and I was about to waste them on a person who would not even appreciate them. Grrrr!

You cannot growl and pray at the same time. I tried but Jesus wouldn't listen. So I humbled myself just enough to grumble to Him.

"Lord, why do I have to waste these brownies on her." She should be baking brownies for me. She should come over here and apologize to me!"

My soul bent under the weight of all the *me's* I was piling upon my crown. Pride and indignation are hideous jewels.

"I don't want to give in to her. I do want to give in to You, but not to her." I could no longer hold up my head before the One with whom I was struggling. "You won't let me do the one without the other, will You?"

There was a long silence in my soul. Not so much a struggle anymore, but a slow, sad releasing. Finally, I surrendered.

"I know, Father. I see how ugly I am. I'm so sorry. Please, You can make me pretty again and help me to look like You when it's time to deliver these brownies. Please do Your work in me again."

My neighbor looked wary when she opened the door. She knew as well as I did that we were in the middle of a battle.

"I was thinking how much I have upset you by letting the dogs mess up the neighborhood with my trash, and I'm really sorry. I'll try to fix up a way so they can't get into it anymore."

She awkwardly stared down at the brownies.

"I baked you something to say I'm sorry. I hope you like brownies."

"Oh, yes, we do!" she said. And then she smiled.

We talked about unimportant things for a while, both of us relieved that the battle was over. We had won. Both of us had won. The very same part of me that had wrestled with God just a few hours before was lit up with warmth and true love for the woman I had been despising. This time I knew my Father was smiling.

I thought about the advice Eldwin had given me. "You have only stopped the irritation. Now you need to go further and return good for the evil you have experienced, and remember to be gentle, for "a soft answer turns away wrath." He had been so right. It made me wish I could go back and be as kind to the girl I had hurt in the lunch line so many years ago. I do not even know her name. I prayed that God, who does know her name intimately, would reach down through the heavens and bless her. I prayed that if she had not become a Christian yet, she would do so soon and that, when we meet on the other side, I will be able to find her and tell her I am sorry.

These experiences with the lunch line girl and Chipper's owner gave me a deeper understanding of Jesus' command to not only love my enemies but to also do things that will bless them. It was a timely lesson, because I was about to collide head-on with an old friend who meant more to me than any lunch line competitor or seldom-seen neighbor.

Some of the folks we had left behind in Buffalo were understandably confused or upset by all the changes Joe and I had made so rapidly. Let us face it. Joining the Mennonites was not like switching our membership from the Catholic church to the Baptist one—it was radical. We had moved far away from the only home any of them had ever known, and that meant we had broken up the family. We refused to wear the type of clothing they wore, go to the amusement park with them, or cheer with them when the Bills made it to the Super Bowl. And they worried about our children. Would they even know what the Super Bowl was? Or the Buffalo Bills? Or pizza? Or their aunts and uncles?

In rejecting the mammon all around us, our friends and family felt like we were rejecting them. They were hurting.

"Why can't you watch television anymore? And why do you wear those ridiculous costumes?" one of them, whom I will call Sharon, spitefully asked. "Jesus didn't dress like that. You used to be so normal. What about all the fun things we used to do together? And what about your poor children? You're brainwashing them; how will they ever know what's normal? You have no right to do this to them!"

In her own pain, Sharon was lashing out at me. Joe and I were, after all, the cause of all this turmoil. Sharon's angry comments were meant to hurt. And they did.

It was hard to think through my own pain as I tried to sort through what had happened to our relationship. In the confusion I heard Eldwin's words again. "Return good for the evil you have experienced. A soft answer turns away wrath."

I bent my head trying to think of how to respond. "Lord," I quickly prayed. "This is horrible! Please help us. Help me to be like You and to say the right things."

Soft words arranged themselves in my mind as I looked up at Sharon with love in my eyes and tears on my cheeks and began to answer.

"I know it is really hard for you that we moved away and joined the Mennonites. It was so nice when we all lived close and could be together all the time. And I know you understand how much I love God. You love Him too. Imagine if God asked you to do something. You would do it, right? Well, Joe and I really believe that God wants us to do some things differently than we did before.

"It's not that we can't watch TV, it's that we don't want to. And we don't have to dress like this, we want to. If you loved me before when I dressed in jeans and a sleeveless top, can't you still love me now that I dress in a way that tells God His wishes are important to me? That's why we have done all this. You wouldn't want me to say no to God, would you?"

"Of course I don't want you to go against God, but I just think you've gone too far. You do a whole lot more than the Bible says to," Sharon answered, her anger beginning to fade.

"I know we do more than the Bible says we have to," I said. "It's kind of like when you join a club or become a Bills' fan. You want to do everything you can to show you're a fan. You go to the games, buy the team jacket, put the bumper sticker on your car. No one says you have to—you just do it because you're a big fan. Well, Joe and I have become big fans of Jesus, and we've joined up with others who are as excited about Him as we are. We dress like fans, go to the meetings, proudly display the bumper sticker—you know what I mean."

"Yeah." She was not supporting what I said, only letting me know that she understood.

"Aw, Sharon, I still love you like crazy. I always will. Will you still love me too?"

"Of course I still love you!" Her face softened a bit. "That's not what this is about and you know it."

"Should I put on a pot of coffee now?" I asked. It was our way of making up.

"Yeah," she replied, this time with just a hint of a smile.

It has been several years since that painful conversation. Sharon has never fully supported our decision to join the Mennonites, but we have learned how to be comfortable around one another again. We do not argue much either. I think that is because we have just learned what topics are best left undiscussed. That is okay though. Respectful silence can go as far as a plate of brownies or a soft answer to say to someone, "No matter what else. I really love you."

9

BUCKING BRONCOS AND GROUNDHOGS

JOE LOVED WORKING AT CLP. He had liked it well enough at the college too, but Christian Light was so much better. It was a ministry for one thing. These were the people who printed our schoolbooks and the tracts that had gotten us here in the first place. It was satisfying to think that Joe could now return the favor to the next person who was waiting to read a bit of the Good News.

Another great thing about working at Christian Light was the workers; they were all Christians! While that might be stating the obvious, it was a big deal to Joe. The boost his co-workers were to his spirit was tremendous. He came home each night with a smile on his face and looked forward to returning in the morning.

"Mornin', Joe," the assistant manager said as he caught up to my husband on the way to devotions one morning. How was your weekend? Is your family adjusting to living in the country all right?"

"Mornin'. Oh, yes! The boys love all the time outdoors and Becky is very happy. Things are tougher for Meghann though. She has left all her friends behind, and it's a lot harder for her to blend in. Seems she's neither a Baptist nor a Mennonite sometimes. It's like she's stuck between two worlds. Her schooling helps though."

"She's what, tenth grade?"

"No, she's been hitting the books pretty hard. She's hoping to graduate before Christmas."

"Graduating at fifteen. That would be something."

The men quieted as they stepped into the large lunchroom. The assistant manager continued on his way to the podium in the front of the room while Joe grabbed a seat in the back row with the other men.

The bell rang and a feminine voice called out a song selection from the ladies row, "336."

The staff sang together, shared a few announcements, and prayed together like this every morning before heading off to their assigned tasks. They also took a few minutes to chat in small groups. Their work was so varied and so far spread across the plant that they might not see one another again until lunchtime. Besides, they were friends and took the chance to visit whenever they could.

Joe worked in the bindery. That was the section of the plant where the printed sheets of paper were cut and bound into books of various kinds.

He had been assigned to a long, caterpillar-shaped machine called the collator. Each segment of the beast held a stack of giant, printed sheets that would, theoretically, be cut, sorted, stacked, folded, and stapled into perfectly bound workbooks. At least that is what they told Joe when they first assigned him to the machine. (There was a reason why this particular job had been available.)

The collator gave Joe no end of grief. It did not seem to understand what its job was—or else it was just too ornery to do it. Instead of sorting, folding, and stapling the sheets of paper, it would more likely miscount, crunch, and eat them!

"You just keep at it," John told him. "The machine is just a bit fussy. Why, with a little more practice, you'll be an expert."

"You probably told that to the last guy who worked on this crazy machine!" Joe answered with a big grin. His boss's encouragement made him want to master the job.

After several weeks of "keeping at it," Joe still hadn't acquired the fine touch the collator seemed to require. It did not look as if John's prediction was likely to come true any time that year. Too bad they did not have a computer position open. Oh, well. Joe was still glad to be working at such a nice place. He was not going to let a fussy old machine ruin his perfectly good days.

My husband's determined good spirits came crashing down one day when he was doing a run of workbooks that should have been enough to keep the warehouse stocked for a long time. He was in the process of moving a pallet which was stacked with several chest-high stacks of loose sheets when the pallet shifted and the pages cascaded to the floor.

Just as Joe was regaining his breath and feeling very defeated, John rounded the corner and caught sight of the disaster. The manager feigned a look of mock surprise, then let out a huge guffaw. That was just what Joe needed. He blushed a deep crimson as he shared in the amusement. All temptation to anger or despair was blown away by the waves of laughter that erupted from the two men. Had an accident like this happened in his job at the college, Joe might have gotten a reprimand, and it would have weighed on his spirits for days. But the mood at CLP was one of camaraderie. Encouragement and shared laughter was just what my husband needed to look on the bright side of things.

Still, it was pretty plain that Joe was probably better suited to work in some other department, preferably one as far away from the collator as possible! So within weeks of the incident with the erupting pallet, Joe was moved to the mailroom. His job there would be to oversee the department and to keep the various computerized and electronic devices running. Ahh, electronics, that was better!

Joe was more of a thinker than a laborer anyway. We both were. Let's face it, he was a computer technician and I had been a chemistry teacher. We were both more comfortable wrapped up in the pages of a book than in garden fence or baler twine.

Our academic bent had actually made it kind of hard for us in our new world where so many of the people were builders and farmers. It seemed at times like they didn't understand us. Many were the times when someone would ask us after church or at a fellowship meal, "So, how's your garden?" or, "Have you tried that new recipe for green beans yet?" I would much rather they had asked me what book I was currently reading or what kind of project was filling my free time. But they didn't. Perhaps they thought academic work was not really work, or at least maybe it was not as good a kind of work as manual labor was. I do not know. In any case, CLP was a place that abounded with thinkers, and we felt very much at home there.

Joe loved working in the mailroom. It was full of people and computers and, you guessed it, books. Still, there were a few ornery machines that intersected his path from time to time. Take the stock picker, for instance. It was a cross between a machine and a bucking bronco—and my husband was no cowboy. As the mailroom staff recalls, the story goes something like this.

The warehouse has two sections. The front section contains the main shelves from which one can quickly pull books to fill small orders. Behind these stand a series of floor-to-ceiling shelves that are used to store piles and crates of inventory that are too big to fit on the smaller shelves.

When the main shelves run low, or an unusually large order comes in, someone has to retrieve the inventory from off the massive storage shelves. This requires the stock-picker.

A stock picker is a very heavy duty motorized forklift with front wheel steering. This allows it to make tight turns into the aisles between the storage shelves. It also makes it extremely awkward to handle for one who does not use it regularly.

Joe was trained on the stock picker, and he could use the machine pretty well, but one day, for some reason, he cranked the steering wheel around too soon when he turned into the aisle. Instead of moving gracefully into the aisle between the racks, the stock picker slammed into a support pole and dislodged it several inches from its previously secure resting place. This was not good.

"Hey, I've done the same thing myself," said one of his co-workers in consolation.

"Me, too," added another. "It can be hard to make those tight corners sometimes."

Neither comment consoled Joe much though. He had been driving the machine when it collided with the support, and he was embarrassed. "Thanks, guys," he said, "but look how far it moved the post. We're gonna have to pull these shelves down and rebuild the entire thing. It'll take days!" It was a gloomy day for Joe.

But he didn't have to commiserate very long, for not too many days later, and before they had found time to rebuild the shelves, Joe was coming out of the same aisle that had been the site of his previous failed attempt to enter. He was, of course, now approaching the support post from the opposite direction when the unbelievable happened. He slammed into the post again!

This was getting to be a very bad habit and not much good for boosting one's on-the-job-confidence.

Joe climbed down from the stock picker, hoping no one had heard him (How can you not hear a motor vehicle colliding with a solid steel shelf head on?) He dejectedly walked around the machine to inspect what damage had been caused this time. To his ever-grateful delight, he found that this second impact, applied from the opposite direction, had reset the post to its original position! Don't ever try to convince me that God does not care about the small things in our lives.

Joe's work at the press sounded so exciting. I wished I had something like that to do. Maybe just a little something intellectual and adultish in the late evenings. I loved the job of raising and training my children, and homeschooling them was extremely fulfilling, but I was striking out so often with my many new domestic experiments that I longed to do something that felt more natural to me—something creative at which I could succeed, maybe something like reviewing manuscripts.

I mentioned my little dream to some of the ladies at a fellowship meal one Sunday afternoon. One of the men in the other room heard my comments and came in to ask me a few questions. As it turns out, he was involved in forming a committee to totally re-write CLP's math curriculum from the ground up. He wondered if I would be interested in being on the committee. I would have to leave home occasionally to be present at the meetings, but any other work involved with the project could probably be done at home.

I could not believe it! It was exactly the sort of thing I had been wishing for. Intellectual, stimulating, valuable, and part time. It was a dream job.

Once I had gotten involved in the math work, other little jobs flitted in now and again, such as a manuscript to review here, an article on homeschooling to write there. And I thoroughly enjoyed it all. It filled a need in my life for a way to use my academic talents. It also gave me a way to earn a little money so I could buy a few of the things that I was not very good at producing myself like fresh garden items and homemade garments. I wrote, others weeded and stitched, and we all got to do what we were best at. It was a nice system.

Sometimes, though, I took on too many jobs at once. Then I would get confused about which department I was working for.

Funniest, I think, was the time I had spent several weeks reviewing a math-oriented manuscript for the curriculum development department. I was grossly absorbed in the project for such a long time that I felt a great relief when it was finally finished.

I made myself a cup of tea to celebrate the completion of the project and quickly faxed off a memo to the department head to let him know I had finished my review.

As I sipped my tea with the satisfaction of a job finally completed, I perused the memo I had just sent off to my supervisor. To my horror, I discovered that my math-saturated brain had written not that I had completed reviewing the first *edi*tion of the manuscript but the first *addi*tion. I was so embarrassed that I wanted to crawl into the fax machine and snatch back the memo. But fax machines, like emails and lips, do not allow one to retrieve words once they have been expressed. Lesson learned: think twice before you speak (or press send).

Now that my youngest child is in high school, I find myself involved with quite a few different projects at CLP. I get almost disoriented when I do not have at least one project calling to me after the supper dishes are finished and the family has all turned their attention to their own favorite pastimes. I call projects like these groundhogs.

See, I have a very close friend with whom I email several times a week. When I was intensely absorbed in a project one time, she said to me, "You remind me of Bowser" (her dog).

"How's that?" I asked.

"When he gets hold of a groundhog, he shakes it and shakes it till it's more than dead. And when he finds it a few hours later he sinks his teeth into it and shakes it some more."

She knew me well. I not only needed a project to grab hold of and shake, but I needed to shake it till it was dead; I could not rest until I knew it was done. And as soon as it was done, I would go hunting up another one to pounce upon.

It makes me wonder what I will do when this book is finished. I have thought of making a coffee table volume of stunning photos from my area of the country. Or maybe I will compile my poetry or finish my family scrapbooks. I would really love to learn how to scuba dive and do an in-depth study of a healthy, thriving coral reef. Wouldn't that be fascinating?

10

THE NORTHERN LIGHTS

ABOUT THE TIME JOE got moved to the mailroom and I started working on the math committee, the two of us were invited to accompany our pastor, Clair Heatwole, and a few other people to visit a small outreach church (now called Lighthouse) on the Canadian peninsula of Nova Scotia. We were to fly out of Ronald Reagan Airport and zip through a narrow layover in Montreal. It sounded exciting.

Beep. Beep. Beep. "Please step over here young man," said the security official at the screening gate to Clair's teenage son, Jared. "Could you empty your pockets into this tray?"

"I don't have anything but my knife."

"You brought a knife on a plane! What were you thinking? We can't let you board with a knife."

The boy looked both cowed and confused.

"But it's my pocketknife."

The guard's expression softened a bit but she still kept the edge in her voice. She had a lesson to teach and the boy needed to hear it.

"Son, knives are dangerous weapons. We don't allow them on airplanes. You will have to either throw the knife into that trash can or stay behind. Which will it be?"

"Throw it away, son," said Clair. "You can buy a new one when we get back. Let's go."

Poor fellow. A farm boy without his pocketknife is a handicapped individual. He threw the knife into the bin with a longing look but without too much hesitation.

He perked up soon enough, though, and by the time we landed in Nova Scotia, he was his old cheerful self.

"Hey, what have you got there?" I asked Jared as he rounded the corner by the baggage claim. I knew very well what it was. I had grown up in Buffalo which is nothing if not the American suburb of Fort Erie, Canada, and I could spot a box of Tim Horton doughnuts a mile away.

"Where'd you find those?" I asked. It had been a long time since breakfast and the bag of complimentary airplane peanuts had not fooled me. I was hungry.

"Just past the bookstore over there." Jared pointed to a small kiosk not far behind him.

"Come on, Babe," said Joe, "let's go get some coffee."

"And doughnuts," I hurried to add. "We mustn't forget the doughnuts."

"Any of you guys want some coffee and doughnuts?" called Joe to our hungry companions waiting in line at the baggage claim. "It's Tim Horton's—best in the north!"

"Tim Horton's!" exclaimed Clair. "Bring me one of everything!"

While Joe and I went off to fetch doughnuts and coffee, Clair and the elderly bishop who was in our group went off to pick up our rental car. They were disappointed to find that the dark vehicle we had reserved had been mistakenly given to a previous customer. All that was left for us was a flaming red mini-van.

Now the mini-van part was fine for we had a large group. But the red was a bit more flashy than the bishop was comfortable with. He had been taught that red was a proud color, and he did not want to tarnish his testimony by driving a flashy vehicle.

Joe and I had run into this sort of thing before when we first moved to the Valley. I have a bit of a problem with my vision that made it hard for me to spot my young boys when they were any distance away from me. A great solution, we had found, was to dress them all in little red baseball caps which I could see from quite a ways off. They never went anywhere without their little red caps.

"I suppose you'll be getting your boys some new caps now that you're with us," said a Mennonite neighbor to Joe soon after we had moved to the Valley.

"Why would we want to do that?"

"Because they're red," he answered, apparently assuming that his answer was an explanation.

"Is there something wrong with red?" asked Joe.

"Well, it's proud, you know; Christians shouldn't wear it."

He said it like he was quoting a Bible verse. How could we not know that?!

Neither Joe nor I found red to be proud or humble—it was just a color. But our new neighbors were obviously offended by the color.

"Joe, you know I can't see the boys very well without those caps. Is it really smart to get rid of them just because someone else thinks they represent something that they don't?" I asked when we discussed the subject later that evening.

"Well, I do think we should do all we can to avoid offending someone else's conscience, and he's our literal neighbor," said Joe. "Yeah, maybe we should get different caps."

So we bought new caps. I still don't know if we made the right choice, but I am comfortable that we made the choice that seemed to be most loving at the time and that counts for a lot.

So here we were, facing the same issue with color only this time it was on a car, and it involved a man whom we both loved and respected very much.

"Brother," said Clair, with compassion in his voice, "red is all they got and we need to drive something. Will you be able to come along with us in a red vehicle?"

The bishop nodded with true humility. "Yes, it will be fine."

And that was the end of the matter. With absolutely no further comments nor a look of discomfort, the bishop surrendered his strong preferences to the unchangeable circumstances we found ourselves in.

Both his willingness to take a stand for that which he found important and his meekness in surrendering to that which he could not change were an inspiration to me. That bishop has since passed on to that place where all colors are beyond description, and I smile to think of God rewarding him for a job well done.

The first group we visited in Nova Scotia was the fledgling Lighthouse church. Because of our schedule, they held a special Saturday evening meeting in the building owned by a local Protestant congregation.

Their group was small, but the worship service was full of the same sweet spirit of love I had come to enjoy each week at Bethany.

A visiting family with grown children was passing through the area, and they stopped in to worship with us. I was absolutely amazed when the entire family stood up and sang a few songs in four-part harmony. They sounded incredibly beautiful together, and I wondered how they had all learned their parts when they had no chorus director. I sat there and cried as their harmony blended with the looks of joy on their faces. Oh, I wished we could sing like that!

"Joe, what did you think of that singing?" I asked after the service.

"That was something."

"Wouldn't it be neat if we could learn to sing like that?"

"We sing like that every Sunday."

"Yeah, but the whole congregation sings then too, so it's easy to follow along. I mean, wouldn't it be neat to be able to sing like that as a family? I suppose they must all read music very well."

"You and Meghann know how to read music," offered Joe.

"Yeah, but we can only read round notes. This is different. These Mennonite hymnals are written with shaped notes that somehow tell you what you are supposed to sing. They learn it in school I suppose."

"Maybe someday we can find someone to teach us the shaped notes."

We said our good-byes to the Lighthouse congregation and headed off with a map to find the Kleine Gemeinde, a colony of Russian Mennonites on the other side of the island. They were closer to the airport, so they offered a perfect place to stay the night before our departure.

We arrived at the home of Jacob Penner in time to watch the women of the house preparing supper. The way the people in the colony regarded and used their belongings was refreshingly different from the way we did in the States. They seemed to have captured the essence of what it really means to live simply. Every item or piece of furniture in the house appeared to have some obvious purpose. There was little that just sat around on a shelf to collect dust.

Consider the kitchen table, for example. When we arrived, the women had placed it in the middle of the single large room and they were using it as a surface on which to pound out and flour tiny pieces of meat. There were no chairs to encumber their movement. All of those had been practically stacked against the wall. This had been easy since the chairs were the simple, washable, plastic style we use back home to line our porches and patios.

When the meat filets were placed into the sizzling skillet, the stray flour was swept from the floor which was then given a quick mopping. Then the chairs were counted out. One for each diner was removed from the stack and placed around the ample, clean table. The rest were left on the stack. Why remove what you don't need?

The bathroom and bedrooms were as plain as the main room. Simple but nicely painted plywood walls bordered the most basic of furniture. Everything was neat and clean, but functional.

After supper, the chairs were given a quick wipe down and arranged in a circle so we could all visit a while before bed. Our host told us a fascinating story.

He had been working at the local gas station where he usually speaks only English for the benefit of his customers, when he overheard two women worriedly talking together in German inside the car he was servicing.

"I don't know what we're going to do! We're down to $10 and every time I try to use the phone, the operator doesn't understand what I'm saying!" said the older of the two travelers. Apparently, the two women spoke only German and the operator knew only English.

"Have you figured out where we are?" asked the other.

"I know we're somewhere near New Glasgow, but unless we can find the airport or someone who understands German..."

"Excuse me, ladies," said Mr. Penner in German as he leaned down toward the driver's window. "I couldn't help overhearing what you were saying just now. I speak German. Can I help you somehow?"

What a miracle it was, he said, that the women had gotten lost at his gas station in the only German speaking colony that he knew of on the island, and that he was able to help them find their way to the airport.

While we were still marveling at Jacob's story, the phone rang. Jacob threw on his coat and excused himself. It seems that one of the young men of the colony had been driving a logging truck when his load shifted and threw his cab out of control. The roof of the cab had been flattened till it was level with the top of the steering wheel. Surely the driver had been crushed along with it.

When Jacob returned not too long after he had left us, we feared the worst. But the look on his face announced that his news was good. How could that be?

It was another miracle, Jacob said. God had thrown the driver flat onto the seat before the roof came down and he had only minor injuries.

Wow! Things were happening in this place. God was working and the people of the colony were giving Him all the credit for it.

We woke the next morning, a Sunday, in plenty of time to share the single bathroom with the family so we could all get ready for the church service.

The huge congregation sat on plain wooden benches in a cement-floored room and sang in unison from a book of multi-stanza, German hymns without the help of any notes or pitch pipes. The singing was very different from that which had so moved me the day before. But it was just as stirring. And it was not hard to get the hang of the music once you figured out how to pronounce the German words. The tunes just kind of flowed from one note to the next so logically that I found myself singing along after a while. It was exhilarating. I was singing with Christians in another language, and we were all able to sing together. I felt an acute awareness of how Christ's body really is controlled by Him.

The minister kindly preached in English for our benefit. That added to the feeling of belonging that these people had extended to us with every welcoming smile. We stayed as long as we could after the service and truly enjoyed ourselves. But we had a plane to catch, and sooner than we wished we were forced to say good-bye.

I have since learned to know some of the Kleine Gemeinde people who have come to work at CLP. Their lives are somewhat of an uncomfortable nudge to a woman who grew up believing she had freed herself from the love of mammon. My time with them suggests that perhaps I am not really as detached from the glitter of this world as I'd like to believe I am.

11

A MERRY MEETING

WHERE I GREW UP, half the people were Irish. The other half pretended they were. Names like Shanahan, O'Reilly and Murphy used up a full third of the phone book. We had a saying in our town, "If you're lucky enough to be Irish, you're lucky enough." But since Joe was a McGurrin and I was a Noonan, we did not have to pretend to be Irish—we were the real thing.

Needless to say, Joe and I were a bit surprised then when folks in the Valley couldn't even pronounce our last name. *Mic-grooo-win* they would say, or *Mic-yer-in*. Ah, well, it was a fair trade, I suppose, for we had just as much trouble learning how to say Rohrer and Stoltzfus, which by all the phonics I remembered should rightly be pronounced, *Row-rer* and *Stolts-fuss*.

Actually, we did not really care how they pronounced our name as long as they did not say something painful like, "McGurrin? That's not a Mennonite name!"

It was hard enough to be far away from home in a new culture that you were trying desperately to figure out and adapt to without someone pointing out how different you were. It made me want to shout sometimes, "Of course McGurrin is a Mennonite name. It has been ever since we joined Bethany Mennonite Church!"

Ah well, we Irish are proud enough as a group so I can't be pointing fingers. Being Irish in Buffalo was about the same as being Mennonite in Harrisonburg. It meant that we belonged to a big family of people who shared a common heritage and religion. It told us where we fit into the world and helped us feel like we belonged.

Some Catholic parishes were almost all Irish. Those were the churches on the South side of the city where the Irish immigrants had settled in the nineteenth century and where neighborhood life revolved around what was going on each evening up at the parish hall.

I lived on the East side. It was more of a mixed section, white, black, Asian, all staggered among each other in a random sort of way. Joe lived on the East side too.

Our church, like most Catholic churches in Buffalo, was very large. There were three services every Sunday and one on Saturday evening for those who preferred to worship then. Many people were so loyal to their particular time slot that they did not even know the people who attended the other services.

I attended the 9 a.m. service because I was in the folk group that led the music at that Mass. Joe preferred the 8 a.m. Mass because he was an early riser and liked to have plenty of daylight hours left after worship. He would faithfully get up before the rest of his family and walk the fifteen or so minutes it took him to get to church. Forty-five minutes later he would be on his way home again—just in time for the 9:00 crowd to begin arriving. I suppose we might have crossed paths in the transition once or twice, but neither of us remembers meeting the other until the year Joe decided it was time for him to find a wife.

He was twenty-four years old already and had been thinking for a while about what kind of wife he wanted. Shy? Talkative? Hard working? More laid back? He did not think he cared much about those things. What he really wanted was a *nice* girl. The kind of girl that did good deeds and loved God. The kind that liked people and was a good listener. The kind that would be loyal and stick with him. Most of his friends were finding wives at parties or bars, but that did not seem like a very good place to find a nice girl. No, nice girls, he decided, would be found at church.

This presented a problem. Joe was about the only young person who attended the 8:00 Mass, and he did not think he wanted to marry a forty-five-year-old widow—no matter how nice she was. Most of the younger ladies attended the Folk Mass at 9:00. There was an obvious solution to that problem. Joe switched to the Folk Mass.

In between the songs and the prayers, he could not help noticing the ladies in the crowd. It was easiest, though, to observe the girls that were in the folk group because they faced the congregation, and he could watch their expressions. He watched them as they sang; was their heart really in what they were singing? He watched the way they greeted one another during the sign of peace; were they kind and friendly?

As he prayed (and scanned), Joe's attention was repeatedly drawn to the girl in the back row of the folk group— second from the right. She smiled when she sang and even bounced a bit to the music. She seemed to have made friends of everyone, even the priests and nuns. He thought he knew who she was, at least he thought she was one of the Noonan girls. He would have to check it out.

In the weeks when Joe was considering whether or not to ask me out for a date (for he had discovered that I was, indeed, the girl in the second row), a remarkable thing happened to him. He was standing near the front of the church in the handsome new suit he had bought. It was Easter Sunday. Joe was waiting to talk to one of his sisters when the very girl who had taken over his every waking thought walked right up to him and said, as if they were long-time friends, "You look great in that suit, Joe."

His heart pounded in his chest as she smiled at him and then moved on. She had talked to him! What was that she had said? *You look great in that suit.* And she had said his name. Did everyone hear the lovely way she pronounced it—*Joe*.

For Joe it was a moment of confirmation. He had been asking God about dating me, and I had come right up and talked to him!

For me, it had been merely a passing notice. The man did look good in his new suit, and it was a nice thing to compliment people, I thought, so why not tell him how nice he looked. I had no idea what contemplations had dominated his prayers for the past several weeks.

Joe somehow worked up the courage and phoned me to ask if I would like to go out with him for an evening. I said yes. I was not thinking much about the future like Joe was. He was looking for a wife. I was not even sure that I wanted to get married. I was still strongly considering medical missionary work—maybe as a nun—so I looked at the date more as a casual friendship sort of thing.

That first date with Joe put me in a spin. I had never enjoyed a fellow so much. He was kind and sweet and rather shy. He held the door for me and poured my drink and made the most delightful conversation. And he did not talk about frivolous things. He enjoyed books and science and ethics and world events. We talked about religion and our dreams and God's will for mankind—and His will for us as individuals.

Both of us will say that we knew that first night that we were highly compatible and considered that it might, perhaps, be God's will for us to get married. I shock myself even now saying such a thing, but it is true. I, who had never strongly considered marriage, was suddenly swept up by a vision of what it could be like to share my life with someone else. Would he like the mission field too, or would I rather like being the wife of a local man? Would I like trading in my independence for partnership? Could he love me when he knew what a wretched human being I was?

I had never considered questions like that before, but meeting Joe opened before me a whole new set of possible futures. Which one would be mine?

It was only fifteen days after that first date that Joe asked me to marry him. Whoa! I needed to get away and think. I needed time to sort things out and to pray. This was ridiculously fast. Was God asking me to get married or was I just infatuated with the idea of being loved?

"Joe, I need some time away to pray about all this," I told him.

He looked worried. He was so sure already. He had had months to pray before asking me to date him, but for me it was all brand new.

"I just need some time, okay?"

"Sure," he said. "Where do you want to go?"

"Well, there's a retreat at the Catholic Center this weekend. It's four days long. Let me go there, and I will give you my answer when I get back."

Joe says it was the longest weekend of his life. He could hardly sleep for all the worrying and praying and dreaming that battled for his attention.

It was long for me too. I had to wrestle with God and with myself at the same time. I had to sort out my will from His. I had to still my own voice until it was quiet enough that I could hear God's voice.

Joe came to pick me up when the four days were over. He looked anxious and drawn. I had planned to wait until we could drive to someplace more private to tell him about my experiences and what I believed God had decided. But when I saw the worried look on his face, I could not torture him any longer. While he was still several feet away from me I shouted, "YES!"

Joe ran toward me then, or maybe he bounced. But his anxiety had morphed into one great big, bubbly smile.

"Let's go somewhere to talk," he said through the smile that just could not seem to settle down.

"Where shall we go?"

"How about the waterfront. We can sit by the water and talk all evening. We've got lots to plan."

Buffalo sits at the junction where Lake Erie narrows rapidly to run through the strait of the Niagara River and hurl itself over the escarpment at Niagara Falls. People in Buffalo grow up with the water. We fish there, walk along the marina on warm summer evenings, and throw scraps to the seagulls who invite themselves to our picnics. When Joe said, "Let's go to the waterfront," he was saying more than that he knew a suitable place to talk. He was saying that since family memories are made down by the water, we should begin planning our future there.

"You got your calendar?" he asked as we sat on the retaining wall to watch the boats sail by.

"I think. Here it is," I said and pulled the little two-year planner out of my bag.

"Can I see it?" he asked as he held out his hands expectantly. "How long do you need to get ready," he asked.

"Get ready for what?" I replied, truly confused.

"For the wedding."

"Oh. Honestly, I haven't thought about a wedding at all. I mean, I thought about the future but more in a long term sort of way. I suppose we should find out how weddings are done, and then we'll know how long we need. I think people usually take a year, don't they?"

"A year!" Joe said in obvious disagreement with my wise idea. "What do we need a year for?"

"Oh, I don't know. We've only been dating a few weeks. It seems we ought to take some more time dating I guess."

"Could we be ready by September?" he asked. It was the beginning of June already.

It all seemed so overwhelming to me. I had only just gotten an answer from God about marrying Joe, and I had not had any time to ask about anything else. I was also worried about how my parents and friends were going to take the news. Engaged after two weeks and married only three months later? I did not relish the thought of being the object of everyone's worried conversations.

"Becky," Joe said softly but with growing determination, "If God thinks we should get married, then why should we worry about what other people think?"

Suddenly I was unsure of myself. Is this what it was going to be like to share my life and decision making with another person? I was used to making decisions for myself and then doing what I thought was best. What do married people do when they have different opinions?

"Joe," I said, "this is all so fast for me. You have had time to think and plan. I haven't."

It was a very long time until he spoke again. I wondered if he was upset. As I would come to learn, Joe took a long time to say anything. At least it seemed so to me. I was used to speaking before I thought. Then, when Joe did not chime in within five seconds of my last word, I would rephrase what I had just said, certain that he had not understood. It must have driven him crazy!

"I'm sorry. I didn't mean to pressure you," he said what seemed a long while later. "I guess I'm just so excited. Let's talk about other things, and we can pick a date later."

That sounded more comfortable. I was relieved. Joe was not going to roll right over me. He was going to listen to me and consider my feelings too. The conversation after that flowed through and around many topics the way it does with engaged (or newly dating) couples. And by the end of the evening I was even ready to pick a date. As I thought about it, I had come to accept what Joe had said. If it was God's leading, three months would be enough time to get ready— but it was going to be a squeeze.

One of the first things we did was to attend a marriage preparation conference sponsored by the church. The conference featured talks by both a young and an older couple as well as a priest.

The presenting couples spoke on things like communicating honestly, planning for the future, and blending our backgrounds to create a new home. After each talk, we engaged couples would find separate places to write down our thoughts and talk about the topic that had just been addressed.

"I'd like at least ten," I said to Joe with a wink when we met after the talk on raising children.

"Me too," he quickly replied—without a wink. He was serious!

"Really?" I said more hesitantly this time. I was the girl who had wanted to be a medical missionary. But a mother? I was not sure I had the skills a woman needed to be a mother. I did not like to bake cookies, I did not do baby talk, and I hated board games. And who would I hire to straighten their toy shelves or clean up after them when they were sick?

"Do you really want lots of children?" I asked.

"Yeah! It was great having all my brothers and sisters around when I was a kid. I don't want our kids to be lonely."

"Well, I wouldn't want them to be lonely either, but can't children be un-lonely if you have just two? I only have two arms anyway. What if they want to be held at the same time?"

"They don't come in litters!" Joe answered. He was laughing out loud now. But I could tell he was very sincere. "I always imagined I'd have lots of children. What did you imagine?"

"Honestly, Joe, I didn't imagine children at all. I always pictured myself as a missionary or a doctor or a marine biologist. Children didn't fit in the picture. I planned on going off and having adventures. You can't do that with ten kids in your pocket."

We had come to our first unexpected disagreement. And we were going to have to solve this one before the wedding day or rethink our plans all together.

"Hey, Babe," Joe said at breakfast the next morning. (When had he started calling me Babe? I kind of liked it.) "I've been thinking about how many children we should have, and I think

I've got a solution."

"What?" I asked.

"Well, I was thinking how we had let God choose whether or not we should get married, and I thought it would be a good idea to let Him pick our family size too."

"Hmmm. I guess. It keeps us from arguing anyway. But if God sends us ten children, I sure hope He sends you a better paying job. You're going to need a lot of money to hire all the staff I'll need to raise them right." It was my turn to smile.

The conference had been a pleasant time to focus on the really important things. But it flew by way too fast. Now we had to go home and do all the fussy things that friends and family expect when they hear an engagement announcement: invitations and programs, menus and table decorations, dresses and suits, and all sorts of socially demanded fooferall. Couldn't we just elope?

Joe and I were married in a very traditional ceremony in the large sanctuary of St. Patrick's Roman Catholic Church on September 25, 1981. After a service filled with our favorite songs and Bible readings, we practically skipped down the aisle arm in arm as we sang along with the rest of the congregation:

> *Sing a new song unto the Lord;*
> *Let your song be sung from mountains high!*
> *Sing a new song unto the Lord; singing, Alleluia!*
>
> *Rise, Oh Children from your sleep,*
> *Your Saviour now has come.*
> *He has turned your sorrow to joy,*
> *And filled your soul with song.*
>
> —*Don Schute, 1972*

Almost thirty years have passed since we sang those words. Thirty years since we joined our lives together and asked God to lead us as a couple. During that time God has sent us four children and, of course, it is just the right number. His timing was perfect too. Our children were spaced over a period of ten years, so I was given plenty of time to slowly learn the skills I needed to train and nurture them. As you can probably tell, I have grown to love the job.

12

THE OLD FARMHOUSE

WE WERE STILL LIVING in the little house we had rented when we first moved to the Valley when Ralph Landes called on the phone to extend another invitation for us to come stay at his house.

"But, Ralph," Joe answered, "you live only five minutes away!"

Joe could hear Ralph chuckling through the receiver. "Got ya that time, didn't I? Actually, we have a house that's empty that we thought would be perfect for your boys. It's a big old farmhouse with a barn and a little chicken house and plenty of space to roam."

"That sounds great!" Joe said.

"You come on over this evening and I'll show you around. It's the big white house right there at the bottom of the hill from mine and Evie's place."

"We'll be there."

We met Ralph and Evelyn at the farmhouse. They had brought Ralph's mother along. She was a real treat! While Ralph and Evelyn showed us the more practical features of the house like the bedrooms, kitchen and heater, Ralph's mother (Grandma Esther) showed the boys the more exciting elements of the property like the sledding hill, hay mow and central banister. The two tours collided when we came out of the formal living room into the central foyer. I heard giggling and looked up to see the eighty-some-year-old woman helping six-year-old Evan to straddle the banister fifteen feet above my head.

"Evan!" I cried (I didn't think it was polite to yell at a grand-mother). "What are you doing!" (It wasn't a question.)

"Oh, he's fine," Grandma Esther replied, "I taught my boys how to slide down this railing when they were his age." It's fine as long as they slow down before they hit that stopper there."

I looked where she was pointing to the bulky knob that perched atop the lowest post of the railing. I really was not wor-ried about him bumping into that. It was the fifteen foot fall that made my stomach churn.

I looked over to Joe for support. He seemed unconcerned. Ralph? No, he was an ex-slider himself; he would be no help. Eve-lyn? She had already moved on into the library. I followed Evelyn into the library before I had to watch any more.

The house was incredible. The large attic insulated the two lower floors, and the front was shaded by giant walnut trees, so the place was cool and breezy. There were more rooms than I cared to clean and all of them were huge. There were genuine bedrooms for everyone who wanted one and they were all upstairs!

The walls could hold plenty of maps and posters and time lines. The computer, the piano, and all of the art and science sup-plies could easily fit in the remaining space. There was even a little counter by the schoolroom window that would be perfect for a fish tank. Best of all, there was an entire room that we could devote to our large collection of books. I would be able to store all of the picture and reference books way down on lower shelves where the little ones could reach them.

"Mom, Mom," Colin said as he pulled at my jacket as politely as he could. "There's a chicken house! Come look."

Colin had acquired a dozen Rhode Island Reds, and they were all good layers. They shared a small coop behind the garage at our current place. It would surely be nice to have a house all ready for them to move into.

"Wow! This is great!" I said as I let Colin pull me into the sturdily built, two-room chicken house. At least I could see that it was just the sort of thing he would delight in.

"Yeah and look at these roosting boxes! And there are feeders and waterers over here, and check out this ramp. They can even let themselves in at night!"

Sure enough. There on the floor of the front room, just beside the roosting boxes, was a small, square, chicken-sized hole that gave access to a narrow ramp. The chickens could, indeed, enter and exit the house without any help from humans. That would be convenient.

"Momma, Momma, come, come, come." It was Nathan this time. "Come. There are cows!"

I held Nate's little hand as he led me out of the chicken house and over behind the barn. There, around—and in—a small pond in the middle of a fenced in pasture were a dozen or so beef cattle.

"My neighbor rents the pasture there," Ralph said as he and Joe walked up and joined us at the fence. "He raises a few head of beef each year."

"You want to go in and see the steers, Nate?" Ralph asked the wide-eyed boy.

"Naw," Nathan replied with feigned courage. "I like to just watch 'em from here." Ralph gave us a knowing smile, and we let the boy enjoy the beasts from his safe position behind the fence.

"Ralph, I can hardly believe this place!" Joe said after we had finished looking around. "It's incredible!"

"Yeah, I spent many a good year in this place. Of course, it's just an old farmhouse. But it's a good place for young'uns." Needless to say, we moved into the Landes place soon after.

Life had brought so many changes in so short a time it seemed, that I found myself taking comfort in the steady things that came with me wherever we went—teaching the boys, CLP assignments, and laundry. I still had plenty of laundry to keep me busy.

I was enjoying the familiarity of emptying little boys' pockets beside the washing machine one Saturday morning when I was treated to the most delightful collection of assorted trinkets to ever encumber a single pair of overalls. They were, of course, Colin's favorite pair of overalls and this partially explains what I found. Hard as it is to believe (I have trouble believing it myself, and I was there), every one of the following items was removed from one small garment on the same day:

One tinder box, one New Testament, one snakebite kit, an 1883 Liberty nickel, one 1955 and one 1949 sixpence, a 1960 peso, a compass, a handkerchief, two alcohol wipes, three band-aids, thirty twist ties, two slings, two magnets, two pocket knives, four safety pins, one keychain ring, one supply of string on a card, one loose string, one screwdriver, nine spent bullet shells, one empty candy wrapper, one origami game, two sketches, two blank white labels, one emergency fishing line on a mini twig-rod, two memos, one glass gem identified as a piece of Aaron's breastplate, two secret codes wrapped in rubber bands and one rubber chicken!

—Becky's Journal

Needless to say, Colin loved pockets, and with good reason. He needed them! I was delighted when, a few days after emptying the boy's denim treasure box, I found at the store some canvas trousers with pockets not only in front and back, but on the legs as well. I bought him several pair so he would have extra pockets on all of his clothes, not just the ones he wore for working around the yard.

"I noticed your son has taken to wearing cargo pants," said a neighbor soon after I had bought the wonderfully pocketed trousers. I could tell he had some opinion about the pants which I probably was not going to agree with.

"Cargo pants?" I asked. "You mean the ones with the pockets on the side? Yes, he likes them very much because he has plenty of places now to carry all his gear."

"I just wondered if you realized what a statement they make?" he added.

"No, what statement?" I asked. This was starting to sound like the red baseball caps all over again. So many people seemed to have opinions about things that the church had never expressed any problem with. And their opinions did not always agree with the next fellow's. Some thought we should wear suspenders to remind ourselves of who we were, some thought they were a waste of money. Some thought women's hosiery should be black, others thought it should be tan. Some wore bonnets, others wore scarves. It was all so confusing.

I asked Joe what he thought about the cargo pants later that evening.

"I think they're just fine. Why, if we tried to please everyone, we wouldn't please anyone. It's enough if we please our ministers," he said.

That was a comfort. The ministers asked very little of us, and what they did ask made a lot of sense. I wondered if people felt so free to admonish us because we were new. I tried not to let it bother me, though. I figured if God and the ministry and my husband thought things were okay, then I should not worry what random neighbors thought.

We had not been living on the Landes place but a few weeks when cold weather moved in, and we realized that the old farmhouse that was so cool and breezy in the summer was just as breezy, but colder, in the winter.

"My room is freezing!" Meghann said as she descended the stairs in several layers of pajamas.

"Ours is even colder!" answered Colin. He was right, too. The only heat source in the entire house was a small propane heater in the center of the schoolroom. We jokingly referred to it as *central heating*. It was warm enough during the school day, but if you had to go to the bathroom, or get a library book, or try to fix supper, you might as well do it with your jacket on.

The bedrooms were the coldest. The original builder had planned for those rooms to be heated by the individual fireplaces that he had built into each room. But the chimneys were a hundred years old now and too unsafe to use.

"Joe," I said with visible breath one frosty morning. I knew he was beside me because I could see his one eye peeking at me from the mass of comforters on his side of the bed.

"You see that ice on the window over there?"

The eye moved slightly. "Yeah."

"It's on the inside!"

"Yeah." The eye disappeared beneath the covers.

"I'm too cold to even get out of bed." I said. My voice quivered with each shiver, and I was so cold I felt sick. "We can't do this all winter."

Later that day, Joe and Colin hauled all the mattresses downstairs and stacked them out of sight in the library. We shut all the doors except those connecting the school room, the kitchen, and the bathroom. The warmth from the little heater seemed able to warm just those three rooms.

Each frigid night after that, when all threat of company was gone, we pulled the mattresses out of the library and lay them on the floor as near to the heater as they could safely rest. So much for sleeping in our own bedrooms!

It was kind of fun, though. Sort of like being on a long camping trip, or like a visit to *The Little House on the Prairie*. In the morning we studied, in the afternoon we read history, in the evening we ate supper, and then we pulled out the mattresses for another night around the campfire.

"Hey, Ralph," I said one morning as I opened the door to let him in.

"Mornin', Becky-Sue." (My middle name isn't Sue but Ralph was like my Dad away from home so I let him call me that anyway.) "Hi, boys. I figured I'd just stop in and look at this here heater on my way to check my turkeys," he said, as he bent down to look at the temperature setting.

"Everything looks fine," he said as he examined the small gauge. I think you might just want to get something that puts out a bit more heat. Course your gas bill will go up if you do."

"Joe's thinking of getting a wood stove," I replied. "He knows where he can get some wood for free if he's willing to chop it himself."

Morning visits from Ralph were not unusual. Since our house was between his place and the turkey barns, he often stopped in on his way back from the barns to check if everything was all right with us at the house. And since he had just been surrounded by twenty thousand very natural smelling birds, he usually brought a bit of turkey smell in on his chore clothes. This morning, though, he had stopped in to check the heater before he went to the barns, so he smelled more like Irish Spring soap than guano.

"Sniff, sniff." Evan walked up to Ralph without embarrassment and stuck his little nose right up to the stooping man's shirt.

"Ralph, how come you don't stink today?"

"How come I don't stink? Do I usually stink?" Ralph asked, surprised but just as un-embarrassed as the boy.

Evan nodded. "Like a turkey."

"Haw, Haw!" Ralph laughed deep and long, his face beaming with delight in this little, candid friend of his.

"You like me better this way, don't you?"

Evan nodded again.

"Well, I'll try to remember that," said Ralph, still laughing.

13

CHUTE!

Joe bought a two-tiered, cast iron, wood stove called the baby bear. It promised to put out a lot more heat than the propane heater. For the next few Saturdays we could hear him out in the yard using a chain saw and splitting maul to reduce several, well-seasoned logs into stove-sized chunks. Whenever he got a big enough pile, he would call the boys out to come stack the small logs in the woodshed beside the house.

The stove put out such a steady heat that we opened the library door most days and the downstairs stayed pleasantly warm. Well, I should more accurately say that the downstairs was warmer in the daytime. One thing we quickly learned about wood stoves is that they need to be fed regularly. Though we went to bed warm enough every night, we did not make it to 2 a.m. before some little dreamer's foot would escape from his warm cocoon and wake him with a chill.

"Dad."

"Hm?"

"I'm cold."

"Okay. I'll take care of it."

Joe got up at least once a night to restock the stove. He tried to bank the wood and adjust the damper in such a way that the large chunks would hover between a burn and a smolder. But if you want heat from a piece of wood, you are going to have to consume the fuel.

Still, Joe didn't seem to mind the chore. He developed a routine: roll over, open the stove, stir things around a bit, and toss in the log he had placed by his pillow the night before. It got to where he could do it without fully waking.

"Hey, Joe," I asked one Saturday morning. "Do you suppose I could cook on that stove?"

"I don't see why not."

"Could I bake in it?"

"What do you want to bake?"

"Potatoes," I said. Feelings of kitchen inadequacy were plaguing me again, and I thought that maybe with a wood stove, I could finally have some success with *plain* cooking.

"I don't see any reason why you couldn't bake potatoes. Just be sure you use the maple wood; I think pine logs might give it a funny taste or something."

I wrapped six big potatoes in foil and opened the door to the wood stove. "Where's the best place to put them?" I wondered. The floor of the oven circling the burning logs seemed like a good place so I arranged the shiny foil packets in a semicircle around the fire.

Several hours later (how long does it take potatoes to bake?) I quick fried some burgers in an iron skillet on the highest tier of the same stove. Maybe I was going to like the simple life after all. This was kind of fun.

Everyone gathered around the delicious smelling burgers and watched expectantly as I opened the stove door to pull out the horribly black and shrunken potatoes.

They did not look like potatoes. The poor spuds had shriveled in the intense heat of the stove and their lengthy stay had literally vaporized any moisture they had once contained. As for smokey flavor, the leathery little nuggets reeked of it.

"Burgers are nice all by themselves," said Joe, trying to encourage me. What a hero! "Bring the buns and ketchup down here on the floor. We're gonna have a picnic."

"Can we go sledding after supper?" asked Colin, mid-burger.

"Yeah!" added his excited little brothers. They stared at Joe as they waited for his answer. They, too, had learned to give their father time to think before he spoke.

"I've got to work on the car. Maybe mom wants to go out with you."

"Tell you what," I said. "You guys help me with the dishes, and then I'll go out sledding with you."

"Will you go on the sled?" asked Colin.

"Oh, I don't know about that. I think I'll just watch you guys have fun." I had long ago learned that getting on a sled was a very dangerous thing for me to do. Where other people seemed able to steer the little plastic torpedoes, I shot straight for the nearest hard object and met it head on.

The chicken house was down the hill about fifty yards from the people house. Between us and it was the most inviting place to sled that our boys had ever seen.

"Whoo-hoo!" screamed Colin as he belly-flopped onto the bright orange sled and made the first run of the evening.

Nathan sat down in front of Evan on the other sled, and I gave them a gentle push. They were not quite ready for a *whoo-hoo* yet. They simply let the wind steal their breath as it rushed into their wide open, smiling mouths. All three boys arrived safely at the bottom of the hill. There was not much else they could do. The path was wide and smooth, and the many previous passes they had made had tamped the snow into a hard, slick chute.

"You try." Colin held his sled out to me. "It's a blast!" Memories of sledding accidents long ago competed for my attention.

I have lost consciousness many times in my life and the first time was on a sledding hill. I was maybe six or seven years old and my parents had taken us to Como Park. It was the best park around for winter fun because it had both a sledding hill and an outdoor skating rink.

Mom always brought along sandwiches and a Thermos or two of hot cocoa. Somehow, she would corral the six of us Noonans at one time so we could share lunch together in the warm lodge. The food was welcome—especially the hot cocoa—but what I really wanted was to stay outside. I figured I could eat at home. Why waste time doing it when I could skate and sled?

At the end of one long, incredibly happy day of winter play my dad said, "You can all take one more trip down and then it's time to go home." He always gave us a warning like that. It made it so much easier to leave.

I stood at the top of the mountain of snow and planned my last run. I had one of those wooden sleds on metal runners. Most of the kids did. The plastic kind were rather new and they did not steer as well. I saw where I wanted to go— over to the left, toward the skating rink. There were not many kids over that way.

"Whoo-hoo!" I shouted at the top of my lungs as I shot head first down the hill. I accelerated rapidly and nothing was in my way to make me slow down or abort my run. It was the most exhilarating ride of the day.

And then a lady stepped into my path. I do not think she saw me coming. She was looking the other way and not paying much attention to me or to the wooden sled she was pulling at the end of her rope.

Thwack! I slammed into her sled and went tumbling. My forehead had collided with the metal runners of her sled and I lost consciousness instantly.

I became aware of my father's voice as he called to me through the haze. I was lying in the snow with his hand cradling my head. He smiled at me, but I could see worry in his face too. My forehead was swelling terribly and he could see it.

Dad carried my sled and helped me back to the car. I guess everyone else had already been headed that way, but he had been waiting for me and saw the whole thing. He said it looked to him like I had veered from an obvious path and had steered straight for the woman. She had been unharmed; I had only hit her sled. I was both sore and humbled. Sledding was a major pastime in Buffalo in the winter. I was going to have to learn to steer better.

Winters came and went and I kept on sledding—and plowing into things. I did not learn to steer any better but I did not knock myself out doing it again until I was thirteen.

It happened when I was at Girl Scout camp. We used inner tubes instead of sleds at that camp. They were more fun. We not only whizzed down the hill at glorious speeds, but we twirled and bounced as we did so. Steering was not an option. How can you steer a rubber ball? It was just the sport for me.

The sledding hill at camp was wide, but it was bordered by thick forest. This did not seem like a problem though because the tubes generally went down the hill in a relatively straight path. All one had to do to keep clear of the trees was start in the center of the hill.

I dragged an extra large tube to the middle of the ridge and hopped on. The tube rapidly picked up speed on the perfectly packed, glassy slope. Faster! Faster! I was twirling and bouncing and I lost all sense of direction until I saw the trees approaching. I knew I was doomed. The tube had apparently, against all laws of physics, taken a sharp left turn seconds after I had begun my descent. I was headed for the forest!

Thwam! Thwam! Slam! Thwack! Thud! I did not pass out when I hit the first tree. I stayed conscious when my head slammed against the trunk of the second one. I was awake for the third. And the fourth. As head then arm, then chest and head again violently collided with one tree after another, I felt a remarkable sense of slow-motion curiosity. There was no pain, just a dull, thudding impact. And then another and another. I only realized that I had been knocked unconscious when I came to at the bottom of the hill.

"Ohhh! I moaned. There was pain now. Though my body had stopped slamming into trees, my head and limbs were still thudding. It is remarkable to me that I did not break any bones. I was bruised and swollen but intact. Before I even sat myself up, I did a very wise and important thing. I decided that I was going to learn to cross-country ski and permanently leave sledding to other, more steer-worthy people.

"You try, Mom," Colin said again as we stood on the hill above the chicken house.

"Honey, I just can't steer those things. They never go where I want them to, and I always ride right into things."

"It's easy, Mom. Just lean left to go right and lean right to go left. That's all there is to it."

I looked at the hill. The boys had gone down it so many times they had worn a deep, sled-sized groove that steered well clear of the chicken house. It would be practically impossible to jump out of that trough. Maybe this was my chance to redeem my reputation.

"All right," I finally agreed. There was nothing down there but chickens and a snow-covered pasture. How could I mess that up?

I sat on the deceptive orange rectangle, feet first. No belly flopping for me.

"Want me to give you a head start?" Colin asked.

"No. I'm gonna go nice and slow."

I jerked forward ever so slightly. The sled stayed put. Good. I jerked a bit harder. With a little more umph, the sled started to move slowly down the friendly hill. Hey, this was not bad at all.

I picked up speed as I zoomed down the hill in the safety of the groove. And then the unthinkable happened. According to eyewitnesses (my boys), I leaned enough to the left to raise the sled up over the right side of the chute. The sled shot out of the groove and sped straight for the corner of the menacingly placed chicken house. It was the forest all over again!

Panicked birds politely made way as I slammed into the vertex of their sturdily built home.

"Momma!" Nathan cried from the top of the hill.

"Are you all right," asked a worried looking Colin. He had run down the hill as soon as he saw me veer off course and he was right by my side.

"Well, it was a little scary, but I'm not hurt at all."

"Wanna go again?" Hadn't the boy realized how close his mother had just come to orphaning him?

"Are you nuts?" I said it with a big smile. "Of course I do. That was a blast!"

We marched up the hill together and I got on the sled again.

Colin was eagerly instructing me in the correct way to avoid a repeat performance. "You leaned left, Mom. You gotta not lean."

"But what if I start to go that way anyway? What should I do?"

"Lean right. Just remember, if you start heading for the chicken house, lean RIGHT!"

I scooted slowly forward again. I had gotten back on the horse after twenty-five years of sledding abstinence and I fully intended to enjoy myself.

"Whoo-hoo!" I was in the groove and accelerating rapidly. "Whoo-whoooooah!" The sled jumped the track at the same spot as before. I frantically leaned. To the left. Then the right. Which way was I supposed to lean?

Slam!

"You okay, Mom?" This time they all called in a chorus from the top of the hill.

"You okay, Babe?" Apparently Joe had come over to watch just in time to see my little stunt. I brushed the snow off my dress, picked up the sled again, and reassembled my dignity.

"Yeah. It's just this chicken house keeps jumping in front of me every time I try to sled down the hill." We all laughed.

"Boys, come here." Joe called as he led the boys into the chicken house. They came out dragging a hay bale. Joe instructed them how to pile the hay around the corner of the chicken house to make me a soft landing pad.

"Okay, Babe," he said when the hay was all arranged to his satisfaction.

Though I tried desperately to drive the sled straight down the groove, the vehicle had a memory and a penchant for hurling helpless women into buildings. But I did not care. The hay made as soft a landing as any flying sportsman could want, and the impact this time was practically pain free.

"Well, boys. Do you believe me now?" I asked with a full laugh. "My sledding is about as good as my biscuits. Tell you what. You guys can finish the sledding and I'm gonna go in and curl up with a book on the soft, immovable couch."

14
TUMBLEWEEDS

THANKFULLY, WINTERS ARE NOT very long in the Shenandoah Valley. Spring eventually came and the warm weather returned. We officially opened the windows that hardly needed our help to let in the breeze. The sights and sounds that greeted us were delightful.

The first thing I noticed were the bluebells and crocuses that Grandma Esther had sprinkled throughout the lawn when she had lived here so many years before. Then came the daffodils and the tulips, and then the lilac bush flowered and the peonies. There was even a rose bush! It was just as pretty as the ones at Vera Rose's.

There were sounds that came in through the windows too: cows and geese and tractors and the rhythmic beat of horses' hooves as they pulled buggies filled with waving neighbors. Clip-clop. Clip-clop. Clip-clop, they echoed as they climbed the hill in front of our house. You could always tell when the horses reached the top of the hill, for their pace would pick up and their clip-clopping would quicken into a joyful trot.

I sat on the porch swing one afternoon waving to my passing neighbors and marveling at how pleasant my days had become when Joe slammed the front door and plopped down beside me. He was visibly upset.

"What's the matter?" I asked, not really wanting to hear what it was that had made him so angry. I knew he had been stewing over a decision that had recently been made by the conference. Without going into the details of the decision, I will just say that it was one that was very near to my husband's heart, and he was displeased both with the decision and with the way the matter had been handled. He sat beside me for a long time before he finally spoke in tones that were not at all comforting.

"I can't believe they're actually going through with it! It's just not right! Becky, this church isn't what we thought it was. Maybe we need to move!"

I was speechless. Leave the church that I loved so much, the place where our children were learning how to live for Jesus, the place where my soul was finally at home? Could he really mean what he was saying?

"Oh, Joe," I said after a long, long silence. You don't mean it, do you? Where could we go?"

More silence. So much silence, in fact, that I was afraid Joe would never speak again.

"Joe, please! Where would we go? There is no church like the Mennonites. We looked for years. Would you give up all we have because of one decision? What about the boys?"

Joe got up from the swing without speaking and went into the house. I knew better than to follow him.

"Oh, Father!" I cried in my spirit. "Oh please, please help him. Please lead him well and let us stay here. Please."

I did not know what else to pray. I felt so dependent, so helpless. Almost all of my memories included God, and my journey up to this point had always led me closer and closer to Him. Would we turn back from that now?

My thoughts whirled, and I found myself pondering where I was going and where I had been.

I had been so happy growing up in the Catholic church that I had never considered moving to a different church until after Meghann was born. It was not until the time Joe and I were charmed by the sweet little voices of our Protestant neighbor children singing, *Jesus loves me, this I KNOW,* that we even imagined such a move was possible.

We wanted Meghann to be able to sing songs like that and to think about Jesus while she was yet a small child. But children in our church did not begin Sunday school until they entered first grade, and that was more of an academic thing anyway. I guess I could have taught her children's songs myself if I could have learned them first from someone else. But who would teach me?

As we drove by the other churches in the neighborhood, I wondered what their worship was like and if they taught songs like *Jesus Loves Me* to little children. I wondered if they believed and loved God like I did. And I wondered what it meant to belong to a church that was not part of the Roman Catholic body around the world. How could I know what God thought of all those other denominations?

It is funny what God uses sometimes to communicate with us, for it was not a pithy saying on a church sign or deep thoughts about doctrine that finally caused me to consider actually visiting one of those mysterious Protestant churches on a Sunday morning. It was not the fact that the preacher believed that the Bible was literally true. It was not even the similarities between their worship style and ours. We were ignorant about all that. It was the way the snow clung to the bricks on the corner of the stately little building of Kensington Episcopal Church.

I had been pulling two-year-old Meghann on the sled behind me. We were just out for an afternoon walk, and on a whim I turned onto a side street that I had never gone down before. I do not remember what I might have been thinking about at the time, but my thoughts were abruptly interrupted by the charming beauty of a small Tudor church building that looked more like it should be nestled in a Thomas Kinkade landscape than squeezed between houses on the corner of Kensington and Blake Streets.

I wonder what it is like inside? I thought. I lifted Meghann from her sled and carried her up the flight of cement steps to the richly polished wooden doors. What in the world was I thinking? You do not just walk up to other peoples' churches and let yourself in in the middle of the week! I felt almost like a thief putting my hand on the brass latch. But I just wanted to see inside. Maybe I would even meet with God there like I sometimes did on walks that drew me into my own church building. The door was locked. I was so disappointed.

"Joe," I said that evening. "I saw a church today that I think I would like to visit. Do you think we could go there on Sunday?" I'm sure he thought I was referring to another Catholic church— what other kind would we go to?

"It's Episcopal." I said after a pause.

Joe looked at me. He was not just taking a long time before he answered. He did not say anything at all. I waited a long time expecting him to at least ask why I wanted to visit a non-Catholic church but he did not.

"Can we go?" I asked when I could wait for his answer no longer.

All he said was, "Yes."

In retrospect, we would both say that God was leading us, but we cannot explain why we were willing—no, planning—to visit a different church. We just wanted to go, so we went.

I felt conspicuous and a bit sheepish when we pulled up in front of the Episcopal church, kind of like a kid hoping no one catches him skipping out of gym class.

"Hello," said a couple who passed us on the sidewalk. They were apparently going into the church too, and they seemed to be quite comfortable about the whole thing. We followed them. This time the door was open and we walked right in.

I was very surprised when I finally got inside the building that had held such a mysterious attraction just a few days before.

Everything looked so normal! It was just a smaller, warmer version of my own church. The familiarity turned out to be very good though. It made it easy for me to worship; I was not distracted by overly foreign surroundings.

The service was familiar too—amazingly so! Many of the prayers were identical; the priest wore the same kind of clothes; the candles gave off the same warm light; even the carpeting was similar.

After the service, we went down to the basement for Sunday school. Now here was something new. Meghann happily accompanied the other children as they followed their young teacher to their classroom. Joe and I stayed in the main room with the other adults, but we were close enough to the children's room to hear their happy little voices recite verses and answer questions about the Bible story their teacher read to them. And we heard them singing.

The adult class was fascinating. All of the students (except Joe and me) had brought their own personal copies of the Bible, and they took copious notes as the pastor led us in a continuing study of the Book of Genesis. But it did not feel one-sided like the sermon had been. It was more informal than that. It was more like how we would interact if we had gathered around someone's coffee table.

"I liked it." Joe said on the short drive home that morning. "I think we should come again."

"Oh, yes!" I added enthusiastically, as though I had to convince him to keep on believing what he had just said. "The pastor is amazing. I couldn't believe how he just quoted one Bible verse after another from memory. And I loved the Sunday school class. But we'll have to bring Bibles next time, and notebooks too. Did you notice how everyone took notes? Some were even writing right in their Bibles! I was surprised at how similar it was to St. Patricks; it's almost like Episcopalians are just another kind of

Catholic."

But I did not have to convince Joe of anything. He had been as excited as I was about the things we had found at Kensington—the familiar style of worship, the engrossing Bible study, the children's ministry. The Episcopal church gave us an ideal place to stand on familiar ground as we reached out to take hold of all the new and wonderful things God wanted to show us.

The first couple of years at Kensington were like a spiritual honeymoon. Normal life was overtaken by a newly awakened sense of God's presence in our lives. We soaked up the Bible studies, and even bought our own study Bibles and started marking them up like everyone else in Sunday school. There were so many exciting and amazing things to record and to talk about later. We bought Bible dictionaries, maps, and concordances and devoured them too. Our little girl was learning Bible verses too, and she was learning to sing. It was such a happy time.

Kensington Episcopal is where we first heard—and became convinced—that the world was created in six literal days. Before that, we had thought that everyone believed in evolution. What else was there to believe? It is also where we came to understand that God is personally involved in our daily lives. We had always believed He was some kind of Benevolent Creator who had set things in motion and intervened from time to time, but who mostly let things run their natural course.

Realizing that God cared about my little daily struggles was the first spiritual milestone I had passed since my days in the Thursday Night Club. I was growing again. It was wonderful!

Joy in this world is never untainted though, and awareness of pain around us eventually dampens the happiest of honeymoons.

"Joe," said my father-in-law in a voice that was at the same time angry and confused and sad. "I know you think you're doing what God wants you to do. And I know you want to raise your kids right. But why can't you do it in the church?"

There, he said it—*the* church. Joe's father thought there was only one real church in the world and that was the Roman Catholic Church. All other Christian denominations were merely disassociated off-shoots. It was understandable to him that someone born in a Protestant church might want to stay there, but for a Catholic to switch was almost sin!

"Dad," Joe said it so gently. "I know this is hard for you; I know it hurts you personally. But I really think that God wants us to go to Kensington. You raised me the way you thought was best, and I thank you for that. Now I have to raise my daughter the way I think is best."

"But why can't you do it in the church?" Joe just could not help him understand.

Things were very awkward at family gatherings for several years—especially on holidays. Mostly, we avoided the topic of religion altogether, but every once in a while Dad would say, "But why did you have to leave the church?"

If only he could understand how happy we were! We were growing closer to God every day; we were learning what the Bible teaches; we were becoming more like Jesus and our home was a place of kindness and love. If only we could have found a way to reassure him.

We attended Kensington Episcopal for about five years, and it was a time of great spiritual growth for us. We will always be grateful for the people there who loved us and taught us how very real and alive God is and how we can trust that the Bible is literally His Word.

Then, about the time Colin was born and Meghann was entering school, we found ourselves hungering for more. Kensington was great on Sunday mornings, but we wanted something else—something that we could take with us through the week. "Did the House of Prayer still hold a Thursday Night Club?" I wondered. And if they did, did they have anything similar for adults?

I found the church's number in the phone book and called the secretary. Yes, she said, they did still hold a midweek program, but now it was on Wednesdays and it had something for everyone in the family. We showed up that Wednesday evening.

When we walked into the main building of the sprawling church, we were amazed to see maybe two or three hundred people sitting at big round tables in the fellowship hall. The church staff had prepared supper like they do every Wednesday. It was the kind of supper my family seldom got. There were several courses of well-made, delicious food and even dessert.

"Say," began the young father seated across from us. He was looking at Joe. "Did you by any chance go to the tech high school on the East Side?"

"Yeah," answered Joe. I could see recognition dawning on my husband's face. "Ken Emerson?"

"Yeah!" answered our dinner companion. "Joe McGurrin?"

"Yeah!"

"Well, I'll be! Who would have believed it!"

"Amazing!" Joe answered. "Do you come here a lot?"

"Pretty regularly. This is mine and Pam's church now. We've been coming here for about three years."

Ken had gone to school with Joe, and he and his wife had been Roman Catholics just like we had. It was nice to bump into old friends like this.

As for me, I felt like I had come full circle. I was sitting in the same building in which I had spent so much time with God as a child, and now I was back again with my own two children.

"Do you know where the children's rooms are?" Ken asked Joe after supper.

"No clue."

"Come, I'll show you. Then you can sit with us during prayer meeting."

The service that night was as strange to us as the Episcopal one had been familiar. There were no fancy priest's robes—there were not any priests! The crowd that had seemed so huge in the fellowship hall looked thin and scattered in the gigantic auditorium. There were no stained glass windows, no altar, no candles. Just a lot of benches facing a wide flat stage.

Ken led us over to a small group near the middle-to-front and we made some new friends while we waited for the service to begin.

Though the room looked strange and barren, I was unexpectedly at ease. I remembered my days in Thursday Night Club and, though I do not think the club had ever met in this room, the spirit of the people was just like I remembered. And even though it did not look like God's room, it sure felt like He was there.

One man led a short study in the Book of John, and then we split into small groups to pray. It was all very informal—even more so than Sunday school class at Kensington—yet it was, at the same time, very reverent.

We returned to the House of Prayer the next Wednesday night, and the next. Before long we found ourselves going there for the Sunday services as well as Wednesday evenings. It was just the right kind of church for our growing family.

Joe and I joined the young marrieds Sunday school class that went through New Testament books verse by verse. Our teacher was incredible, very knowledgeable and on fire for the Lord. In addition to studying the text, he also gave us time to share our thoughts and questions. Couples offered one another practical advice on how to raise our families in ways that would be pleasing to God.

Everything we did and every decision we made centered around Him. Should we have a TV? What would God want? Should we shop on Sunday? What would God want? Should we get involved in neighborhood evangelism? What would God want? Everything boiled down to the question of what God wanted. If we could just discern that, then we would know how to act in every situation.

We threw out all of our questionable games and unhooked the TV antenna so it could only play videos. We began listening to the Christian radio station and bought Christian music tapes that we could sing along with. Some of our friends thought we were changing so fast they mockingly called us tumbleweeds because, as they saw it, we were always rolling from one place to another.

Maybe we are tumbleweeds, I thought. We certainly have covered a lot of ground! Still, the tumbleweed is wise that yields to a Sovereign Wind.

Clip-clop. Clip-clop. The sound of a buggy coming up the hill arrested my journey through the past and brought back the heartache that had come with Joe's announcement that we might be needing to find another church. Would he really take us somewhere else? Where?

The front door opened again, but it did not slam this time. Joe sat quietly beside me and matched my motion on the swing. He took my hand in his.

"I'm sorry, Babe. I'm just so upset. Your question though, when you asked me, 'Where will we go, now?' really made me think. There is no other place to go, is there?"

I looked up at my husband and shook my head just enough to say, no.

"You know," he went on, "it's really amazing when I think of how God has led us. I mean, we tried and tried to get out of the city and couldn't. Then when we decided to do things God's way, He gives us this besides." Joe's hand swept across the horizon as he said it. "We would be fools to walk out on Him and try to do things on our own again, wouldn't we?"

I nodded again. This was not a time when Joe really wanted me to talk. He just needed to work through some things out loud.

It was enough to know that my husband was listening to God even though things were not being done exactly the way he thought they should be. It seemed our tumbleweed days were finally over.

15

UNEXPECTED COMPANY

I T TOOK SOME TIME before Joe's spirit settled down fully. He never did come to agree with the particular conference decision that had upset him so deeply, but he eventually came to accept it. It had been his crisis point, and he had passed the test. I thank God for the trial for it seems to have made Joe all the more convinced that we were truly in the center of God's will. But that did not mean we were done facing trials related to church life.

Joe had been helping me clean up after supper one evening when I suddenly remembered that it was the third Wednesday of the month, and third Wednesday's were the nights we had cottage meetings.

"Hey," I said as I finished putting the ketchup away. "We should call the boys and tell them to wash up. We have cottage meeting tonight."

"Why don't you go get them ready while I finish up in here," suggested Joe.

"Deal!" I answered before he could rescind the offer.

I found the boys in the library where Evan had erected the little tent his Aunt Rhonda had given him for his seventh birthday. Evan was presumably inside the tent, for Nathan was on his hands and knees peeking into the tent and addressing his older brother.

"Evan?" asked Nate in his sweetest voice. "Can I use your tent too?"

"Well, Nate, we're second best buddies; why wouldn't I share?"

In a double effort to both announce my presence and to make sure no problems developed between my two youngest children, I asked, "Evan, who is your first best buddy?"

His little voice answered from within the tent in a tone that sounded like the answer should be obvious. "God."

All was well with my boys.

"You boys can play in the tent tomorrow; we've got cottage meeting tonight and we have to hurry to get ready," I said.

Both boys cheerfully left the tent and followed me upstairs. They loved cottage meetings, at least they always had before.

We met a small group from Bethany at a run-down old home in a shabbier section of town. Old tires, paint cans, and discarded bits of this and that competed for space on the patch of dirt that surrounded the home. A friendly hound wagged up to each of us as we got out of our vehicles.

"Hello. Come in, come in," said our hostess as she warmly welcomed us into the home she shared with her grown son.

"I'm sorry I don't have more places to sit," she said with obvious embarrassment as we squeezed into the small living room and scooted close together on the small sofa and single chair. A few of the teens stood against the walls, and Nathan settled on the floor.

"Let's sing number 35," called out Jared, the song leader for the meeting that evening.

Our hostess smiled with real delight as we sang one song and then another. That is how it usually was at cottage meetings, and it was the main reason we loved going to them. Not to mention that it was a whole lot easier to reach out to our neighbors as a group like this than to go door to door by ourselves.

I guess I must have been really enjoying the songs, for I was singing so intently that I did not notice everyone had scooted to the very edges of their seats.

Somewhere in the middle of the third or fourth song, I looked up to make eye contact with Dianne who was sitting across the room from me. She was smiling as she sang, like she always does, but something about the way she sat caused me to look down at her legs.

And then I saw them. Roaches. The room was crawling with thousands and thousands of roaches. They were climbing up her legs and all around the carpet by her feet. They scurried along the walls and covered the chairs like upholstery. And they were on me.

Nathan was lying on the floor oblivious to his tiny playmates, and Evan was leaning with his head against the back of the couch.

I pulled Evan up to the edge of the sofa as I nonchalantly pretended I did not notice the cockroach on my ankle while trying to whisk it away. Oh how much longer must we stay here? The songs that had been so absorbing just minutes before now dragged on interminably. And then I thought of Jesus. Three hours on a horrible cross for me. Could I not wait one hour with Him?

"Oh, Father," I prayed. "This is unbearable! How is everyone else able to sit so still and to keep on singing?" I knew I had to keep on singing too. There were two lonely souls in that home who needed to hear about the love of God. Would they be able to believe our message if we could not love them enough to spend one hour with roaches for them?

With Jesus as our inspiration and our very real helper, we stayed and sang and shared Bible verses and smiled for the full hour.

Still, our post-meeting conversations were not prolonged. As soon as the last song was sung, we said very hasty good-byes and practically ran out to our cars. There, in the blessed darkness we frantically slapped at one another's clothing, trying to dislodge the vile insects lest any of us bring them into our vehicles. No one thought to brush out our hair.

When we got home, we took turns disrobing in the shadows and running into the house for quick but very thorough showers. This was a real challenge for those who got to bathe last. There was no hot water left by the time the last two got into the shower, so their de-bugging, though just as meticulous, was a mighty chilling experience.

How curious the next morning's early commuters must have been when they drove past our front yard and saw what must have looked like a few loads of laundry strewn all over the driveway, but none of it was near the clothes lines!

Joe gathered the clothes from their scattered piles on the ground and boiled them in a kettle outside. Then we sprayed the inside of the car with disinfectant. We thought that should be sufficient, though we found ourselves scratching a lot from the memories.

Two weeks later, Evan was still scratching. He had caught head lice and the disinfecting began all over again. We sprayed the furniture, washed all the bedding, and sealed stuffed animals and pillows in plastic bags for two weeks (the life cycle of lice). Our poor boy had to be shampooed with some powerful chemicals and get a really short haircut.

Thankfully, most visitors are a whole lot more pleasant than the unexpected company we brought home that night. Transplants that we were, we were very glad that Mennonites love to visit.

You see, it is a lonely thing for people who love their families to move far away to a place where, in a sense, nobody needs them. Most of the folks at Bethany had large extended families, and when church let out on Sunday afternoon, many of them would go off to visit with those families. What did they need us for?

But even though people like Clair's, Ralph's, and Eldwin's and the other folks at Bethany had plenty of extended family too, they often included us in their Sunday noon meals. Could they have possibly known what this meant to us? They must have; why else would they give up the one day of the week they had available to just relax as a family? Had they not reached out to us like they did, the loss of extended family would have been doubly hard.

Still, as is usually the case with blended families, we discovered some awkward and even laughable differences between our two native cultures.

Take food styles for instance. Where we came from, spaghetti in a bowl with a little sauce and maybe a meatball or two was a full meal. But our new Mennonite family never served us just one item in a bowl. They accompanied it with all manner of breads and salads and jello (which they also called salad for some reason) and fruit and desserts. We did not know if we were expected to take a bit of everything or just pile our plates high with our favorite things.

One thing we did learn was that, no matter what you took, you were expected to scrape it all off your plate and eat it. It did not matter if your post-meal plate was covered with a congealing whirl of beet juice, whipped cream and mushroom soup (every entree comes doused with mushroom soup), you were expected to scoop the irreconcilable sauces together onto your spoon and place them into your mouth at the same time. They called it, "scraping your plate." Whew! If we had acted like that at the table back home, our parents would have scolded us for acting like uncultured swine. After all, had we not gotten enough to eat that we had to scrape off and eat the slop?

And the sound of all the scraping spoons on Sunday china was enough to make you want to get everyone a rubber scraper so they could gather up the drippings more peacefully.

But we knew why our new relatives were so intent about their scraping. They were neither rude nor unsatisfied, they were just thrifty. They were grateful for what God had given them, and they wanted to show their appreciation by not wasting any of it—even if they had to experience whipped cream and mushroom gravy in the same mouthful.

Another notable thing about the culinary preferences of our new family was their love of sugar. They put it in everything, even salad dressing. Most of us McGurrins could handle the unusually sweet dishes all right. But Colin, whose palate is pickier than most to begin with, was sore pressed to smile at someone else's table. But he did smile and I don't think our hostesses ever realized what a trial it was for him to eat their carefully prepared blends of lettuce, mayo, eggs, and sugar.

Poor boy, he can barely get mayo past his tongue when it is hiding in a sandwich, and he prefers to eat his lettuce undressed, but he cannot swallow an egg no matter how it is disguised.

I laugh when I remember him sitting across from me at a friend's table after church one Sunday. There were several other guests there as well, but Colin had been given the honor of sitting right beside the hostess. When she passed him the bowl of sugared eggs and lettuce, he looked up at me with a pleading look. I returned the look that he could not help but understand to say, "You bet you need to eat some of that!"

He scooped out the tiniest spoonful and quickly passed the dish on to the diner beside him.

Being the sort of guy who likes to get torture over with so he can enjoy the rest of the day, Colin wolfed down the salad in the first bite—though I'm sure he never let it touch his tongue. He followed the unpalatable mixture with a long gulp of water and turned his attention to the more tolerable items on his plate.

Alas! The hostess beside him, unable to see the struggle on his face, only noticed how quickly he had devoured the lettuce and egg salad. So when it was time for seconds, she picked up the salad bowl and, remarking on how glad she was to see a boy eat so heartily, scooped a giant mound of the dreadful mixture onto his proudly empty plate.

The look he gave me about broke my heart. Had I been beside Colin I could have waited until our hostess was looking the other way and transferred at least some of the salad onto my own plate. But my suffering child was beyond my reach. He was going to have to handle this one alone.

I gave him a look that this time said, "You're a man, son. I know you can do it!"

Colin asked for another drink of water (he was going to need it), turned down his taste buds as best he could, and ate the salad. He has not sat beside a hostess since that day.

16

A STRONG TOWER

"**M**OM, DID YOU HEAR about what has happened in New York?" Meghann asked from the telephone receiver. The panic in her voice was almost palpable.

She was calling me from the office of the little school in Indiana where she had moved just a few weeks earlier to teach a first grader. Another teacher had been hired to teach the older students.

"No, Sweetie. What's going on," I asked, more to calm her down than to find out the news.

"A plane just crashed into the World Trade Center and there might be more planes aimed at other buildings! What should we do?"

I was still processing the incomprehensible statement she had just made when I realized what she had asked me. "What do you mean, do? What should you do about what? Do you know someone who is in New York?"

"Not in New York—here. What should we do about the children? Should we tell them?"

"Oh." I realized now what she was getting at. There were eleven young students in the little one-room school. The two teachers themselves were barely out of high school and had never been through a crisis like this before. How were they supposed to help their students?

"Oh, man!" Meghann cried into the phone. "They just slammed into the second tower. They're both on fire!!"

There was only one thing I wanted at that moment and that was to drive straight to Indiana and bring my daughter home. The country was facing a collective crisis, and all of my mother instincts screamed for me to "go!"

But I did not go. Nor did Meghann come home. Instead, we did what most other people did that mind-numbing day in September of 2001. We turned to the people who were right beside us and hung on. Meghann gathered with her students and their families at their small church in Indiana and I hit the streets in Harrisonburg, Virginia.

Joe and I thought that as there were probably thousands of people within a few square miles of us who were dazed and searching for something to help them make sense of the chaos around them, we needed to find them as soon as we could. Cracks—no, gaping holes—had been blasted into the walls of their once-secure existence, but no light was shining through. We knew the Light personally, and we wanted to help them see Him too.

We called around and found a small group of people who shared our desire to get out into the community. CLP offered to give us as many *Just for You* tracts as we could give away, so we all met at CLP to load up our backpacks and plan our strategy.

We decided we would drive down to the university/downtown area together and see if there was anything going on down there. There was. Hundreds of people were out, sitting, biking, driving, aimlessly walking. No one seemed to be going anywhere, they just did not want to be alone. Humanity had been forced to face his vulnerability and he was terrified.

Our challenge was not going to be finding people to minister to but deciding who to approach first. That problem soon solved itself, though. The people came to us.

"Ma'am?" the young fellow in the sweatshirt asked hesitantly as he approached. "Is that information about the Towers you got there?"

"Yes," I answered as I held out a tract to him. "It talks about how God can help us when horrible things like this happen and nothing seems to make sense anymore."

"Does it cost anything?" he asked.

"No, it's free. Here."

"Thanks. I really appreciate it," he said as he took the tract.

The men in the fire truck which was waiting at the red light saw the exchange and called out to Evan who was standing beside me waving tracts to passers-by. "Hey, little boy! Hey! Could you bring me one of those?" Evan looked up at us. The truck was out in the center lane and the light had just turned green.

"Just come out here and I'll reach down for one." The desperate pleading in the man's voice was heart wrenching; fire fighters had been hit worse than any of us.

"Come on," said Joe as he put his arm around Evan's tiny shoulders and led him through the inching traffic to the waiting truck. Evan stood on tiptoe and stretched his arm up to make contact with the man in the turn-out gear who was leaning out the window, reaching down for the answer he hoped the little boy was holding.

"Thank you," he said. "Thank you." He was crying.

Other drivers stopped and honked their horns or called from their windows. They all wanted to talk or wave or receive a booklet. The policemen did not stop us even though we were in the middle of the street. They came up and asked for literature too. There was no pretending that day.

The daze continued for several months after the attacks on September 11th. People wanted answers. CLP recognized this and combined with other conservative ministries and churches to arrange for weekly trips into New York City. The idea was to go to the place where the people had been hit most directly. The place was called Ground Zero.

We were supplied with pocket-sized Gospels of John and tracts that were tucked into CD's that had been especially recorded for the people in New York. Blazoned across the front of the CD case was the message, "To New York with Love."

Joe and I were invited to go on one of the New York trips in early January, four months after the towers had fallen. Enough time had elapsed for the initial shock to wear off and for the city to return to its pre-September routine, but people were still in deep grief and confusion. Exhausted recovery crews and clean up teams worked amid the smoldering ruins of the collapsed buildings like mindless ants doing their jobs, not because they understood why, but just because they had no other choice. The other millions of the city's occupants wandered in little trails around them, stunned and somber.

A constant stream of pilgrims from around the world swelled the crowds of silently weeping people who stood beside the acres of smoking debris and gazed up at the hole in the sky. Had the towers really been there? The clouds didn't seem to remember them.

The multiple thousands of CDs that had seemed so heavy when we had loaded them onto the bus were pitifully too few for the hundreds of thousands of people who wanted them. When John pulled a box off the bus and set it on the ground to open it so we could refill our backpacks, the groups of waiting people would surround him with eagerly outstretched hands. We sometimes had to limit how many CDs we distributed in a particular area so we would have some left for the people in other parts of the city.

The air was cold in January, and it snowed intermittently the weekend we were there. The sidewalks were as hard as ice. Our faces were chapped, our fingertips were red, and our feet were pounding. I was grateful for the break we got when we descended into the subway. It was warmer down there where there was no wind other than the breeze that always whips through the tunnels.

Beneath the streets, where one's view was shielded from the altered skyline, it was easier to pretend things were still normal. The forty or so of us who had come on the trip would walk along the corridors until we found some busy crosswalk where several hallways converged. There we would arrange ourselves into a small chorus and sing the songs we had come to know mostly by memory. While we sang, the group leaders would call out for a few of us to split up and hand out CDs to the people who were passing by.

In the anonymity provided by the dim lighting and ever bending walls, people seemed to be especially willing to stop and talk a while. Team members listened to them, prayed with them, and offered counsel when the Spirit led. Many people made new or renewed commitments to renounce sin and follow Jesus instead. Others just stopped to listen to the music and have their spirits lifted for a while.

When we wanted to cover a lot of ground, we became commuters ourselves. We would huddle together and try to get all of our team members onto adjoining cars of the same train. Once aboard, we would find ourselves face to face (or side by side) with what you might call a captive audience. Sitting beside someone offered a unique opportunity to have a more prolonged conversation.

The face of one young passenger is burned into my memory. He was maybe 17 or so, a rough looking street kid in a leather jacket. We were sitting beside one another in a dingy subway car somewhere beneath Manhattan. I caught his eye and asked him if he wanted a free CD.

"Is it Christian?" he asked. Odd way to phrase the question, I thought.

"Yes," I answered, "would you like one?"

"Yeah! My mom is a Jehovah's Witness and I never got to have any Christian music before." He said it in the way a child might who had been deprived of candy his entire life.

"Oh," I said with a bit of hesitation. "I don't want to come between a boy and his mother."

"Nah, it's okay. I'm old enough. She'll let me choose for myself now." He looked at me expectantly. Was I going to let him have that first gumdrop?

"Okay," I said and handed him the CD.

"Thanks!" He softly ran his finger over the words on the cover. "To New York with Love."

"Yeah, it really shook us up when the towers fell. We wanted to help somehow. We figured coming here to help people reconnect with God would be the best thing we could do."

He tucked the CD carefully into his bookbag and told me how he did not have his CD player with him or he would listen to the music right away; but he would listen as soon as he got home.

We were so absorbed in conversation after that, that it surprised him when the train driver announced his stop. He got up from his seat, said good-bye to me, and hurried toward the door. Just before he stepped out onto the platform, he turned to look at me one last time. He held up his bookbag as if to remind me of the treasure he had tucked inside. Then a smile covered his handsome face and he said, "Thanks." And he left.

I smile when I think of that boy. I suppose he must be a man by now. Maybe he has a family. If so, I hope they all enjoy the CD. I hope they all love God with their whole heart and soul and mind and strength. And I hope his mother has come to love Him too.

New York City was not very different from Buffalo in a lot of ways. It was like one gigantic downtown, and I knew how to act downtown. Mind your own business, do not invade someone's personal space, and do not make eye contact. My traveling companions did not seem to know these rules. For so long now, I had been adjusting to their world. But now, our roles were reversed, and I looked on with empathy as they tried to make it through the foreign culture that had always seemed so normal to me.

I thought we were in for trouble when John's wife, Ruby, boarded the train, looked straight at the woman who was engrossed in a book on a bench beside the door and said in her friendliest Valley-voice, "Well hello; may I sit here?" The commuter properly ignored the rude interruption from the woman who obviously did not know any better.

Ruby did not seem to notice the put-off. She sat down and continued just as if she had been engaged in a two-way conversation. "Isn't the weather lovely today?"

This got a reaction. The reader looked up from her book and said to the incessantly intrusive, but friendly woman beside her, "Ya ain't from around here, are you?"

"Why, no," responded Ruby in a tone that seemed to imply that she could not imagine how her new friend could have known that much about her when they had just met.

The hardened face of the commuter softened a bit. Her new bench-mate may not understand subway etiquette, but she did not seem to pose any threat. She was not selling or stealing something, and she didn't want to argue. If anything, she seemed like a child. At least the way she had presumed to be friendly to a stranger was childlike. And she was so sweet.

"Do you ride the subway often?" asked Ruby.

"Every day—well, every workday." The response was short, but the tone was friendly now. The conversation had become two sided.

When I looked up a while later, the commuter was holding a CD and both women were talking as if they had known each other for a very long time. It was like that all over the train. At every stop, new people were greeted and welcomed into what seemed to be our own private train car.

Then someone started to sing. It began so quietly that you could not really say who had started first. Maybe someone had been softly humming. Then, without realizing it, someone else had added a few shy words. A few words from the front of the car. A few more from the center. The music had a life of its own. It swelled and harmonized and flowed throughout the group until the entire car was filled with glorious music.

Some of the commuters put down their newspapers to listen. Others hummed along, or sang the words if they knew them as one song followed another in a beautiful, unbroken medley: *Does Jesus Care? In the Rifted Rock I'm Resting, Amazing Grace—How Sweet the Sound!*

I was actually sad when the group leader announced that we would be getting off at the next stop. We were in the middle of a revival meeting! But trains do not wait for revivals.

As we made our way to the doors, people from all over the train waved their hands or their CD's in farewell.

'Thank you," said one.

"God bless you," said another.

"Take care!"

A blast of icy wind greeted us as we climbed out of the subway and stepped onto the unsheltered streets of Chinatown. The sun was gone too. We had been singing in the tunnels and riding the train so long that evening had fallen on the people above ground and we had not noticed.

"Brrr," I said as I tucked my hands into my pockets.

"There are a couple of inches of snow up here already. It didn't seem like we were down there that long," added Joe.

The many colored lights of the densely crowded shops lit up the streets like a child's toy. It looked like Christmas time in Buffalo, with people walking together past stores whose twinkling lights glittered between the flakes of falling snow. The atmosphere blended with happy memories and made my spirits light.

And then my heart skipped a beat. There, in window after window, nestled among shoes and lanterns and trinkets of every kind, were ceramic statues of a smiling little man whose round belly hung over his little folded legs. Incense was burning before many of the statues. They were idols of Buddha.

My holiday mood instantly vanished. The colored lights all around me weren't Christmas lights twinkling in the snow; they weren't celebration lights of any kind. They were just brightly glowing tubes of neon that said in some strange tongue, *Come, buy your trinkets and idols here!* It was night in Chinatown. I felt lost and unsure.

We were on our way to a tiny restaurant that our host had reserved for the group. The subway had taken us far across the city, but it did not go quite as far as the restaurant. We would have to walk the rest of the way.

The blanket of snow that had already accumulated on the sidewalks softly cushioned our tired feet, and we were grateful for that, but the storm was worsening and it was getting harder to see. We were going to have to stick close to the people in front of us and not stop too long at any of the shops.

This presented a problem for Joe and me. We had been assigned, along with one other fellow, to make sure that we were always the last ones in line. The rationale was that if we did not let anyone fall behind us, no one would be lost in the big city. We, at the tail, might still get cut off from the group, but we would have each other. This had already happened a few times over the weekend.

One member of our group was particularly zealous about his evangelistic efforts, and he could not bear to pass by someone without first making sure they were given at least one chance to come to know Jesus. I will call this steadfast worker Philip. We had already been cut off from the group twice that day because Philip was in earnest conversation with some interested pedestrian. He got so absorbed in his conversation that he did not notice the group steadily filing past him. Eventually, we would catch up to Philip and stop. We could not go on without him, but neither could we interrupt his conversation. What could we do?

So we just stood there and waited for him as the group went on without us. Of course they thought we were with them. We had been assigned to make sure that no one got behind us, but no one was assigned to make sure we were not left behind!

It was not a big deal though. When the main group took a head count at the next stop (just as they were about to board a train), they would notice they were short a few heads and send someone back to find us.

But this was night, a dark snowy night now, and we were walking through a very congested and unknown area of the city. We could not even read the signs. They were in Chinese. If we got separated here, how would anyone ever find us?

Then again, maybe we were not at much risk of being left behind here. Philip did not speak Chinese, so how likely was it that he could lose himself in a conversation with someone?

Philip did not need to speak Chinese. He apparently had the gift of tongues; that or his smile said enough. We had not turned the first corner before he started a conversation with a small man in one of the corrugated steel shops that were beginning to close up for the night.

What could the two men possibly be saying to one another I wondered as the main group disappeared into the thickly falling snow? They were both smiling and nodding, but they were clearly speaking two different languages! It was not long before the shop-keeper held up a pair of fingers in a gesture that indicated *two* in any language. Philip nodded and handed the smiling man two CDs. The shopkeeper nodded in thanks, and Philip, content that he had made another successful contact, stepped out of the steel box with a similar smile and a wave.

We looked in the direction we had last seen the group. There was nothing there but millions of tiny snowflakes sparkling in the glow of the street lights. Even the neon lights had disappeared. Many of the shops were closed now. We used the curb as a guide and walked a few yards in the direction our companions had gone and nearly stumbled into the street. We had come to a corner. Had the group continued across the street or had they turned the corner? Or maybe they had crossed to the left.

The unease that had begun with the Buddhas in the windows and the sounds of many foreign words spoken around me was coalescing into real panic. We were truly lost this time, and no one would even understand our request for help!

We stood on the corner and wondered what to do. "We'll just stand right here till they come find us," said Joe, with not a hint of panic in his voice. "They know where we are and there's no sense our walking off and getting lost."

Getting lost? I thought we were lost! Joe always looked at things like this in such a strange way.

"There you are!" said a friendly English voice from the fog to our right about twenty minutes later. "Thought we lost you for good this time." Our leader was grinning from ear to ear, but he did not seem at all surprised to find us on that particular street corner.

"I was beginning to wonder what it was going to be like to sleep out the night in a cold, snowy alley," I said, returning his grin in a way that, I hoped, looked as playful as his.

"Aww, I wouldn't let you do that." His big, warm smile was like a big, welcome home sign. "Come this way. They've got the food all ready for us."

17

BORROWING AND BUTCHERING

SPRING CAME AGAIN TO the Valley. We had lived here four years already and felt like we were finally starting to understand who we were in God's sight and just how it was that He wanted us to fit into His kingdom. We were an academic and technically oriented family with some strange city-bred habits living in one of the most traditional sections of the American farmland, but folks did not seem to mind us that way.

Yet for all of their acceptance, we were still a bit uncomfortable. In our hearts we wished we could be a little bit more like the people we lived and worked among. Doesn't everyone wish to be like their peers?

Folks at church were so industrious and hard working, and they knew how to do so many things! Why couldn't we be like that?

The struggle between accepting ourselves as we were and striving to grow and learn ebbed and flowed. But it hit a new high when Joe began wishing he could have some animals to work with. Colin did have his chickens, but they were not really like animals. No, Joe wanted something big like a horse or a cow.

"Honey?" I asked him when the farmer mood struck him pretty hard one day. "What would you do if you did have a cow?

You don't know how to milk one and we'd have no place to keep it. Besides, you'd have to milk it every day."

"I know," he answered with longing in his voice. "I'd like to milk it every day. That's what I'm looking for. A little bit of farm work that I could do every day. Mr. Wenger said he'd let me keep a cow in with his herd. And you could have all the milk you wanted."

"I don't know. Cows make a lot of milk."

"John keeps a cow for milking. I'll ask him about it."

Joe caught up with John in the lunchroom at work the next day.

"Hey, John, you guys keep a milk cow, don't you?"

"Yes, why do you ask?" John had a suspicious gleam in his eye when he answered. Now what was that all about?

"Well, I was thinking of maybe getting a cow, and I wanted your advice."

"Have you considered borrowing one for a while to see what it's like. Then you'd know better if you'd really like to own one." There was that gleam again. And was that a little grin forming at the corner of his mouth?

"Borrow a cow? Where could I borrow a cow?"

"Well, it just so happens," said John, whose smile was now full grown, " that I have one I'm needing to lend. You see, I'll be going on a trip next week, and I need someone to look after Old Red. I could bring her to your place, and you could try her out for a few weeks."

"That would be great!"

So it was that a few days later a beautiful red-horned Guernsey came to live in *our* barn.

Joe absolutely loved working with Old Red. Twice a day he went out, spoiled her with some grain, and talked to her as he gently convinced her to give us all the milk she had.

But I think he must have spoiled her too much for she gave out way too much milk for our small family. I did all I could to use the milk like I thought a good farmer's wife would, but we got tired of ice cream, and the cheeses I tried to make were threaded through with a disagreeable looking mold. I suppose I might have discovered the next best thing to Roquefort, but we were not adventurous enough to try it.

My funniest memory from the days we had Old Red was the time our barefooted young Nathan, who was now seven and had gathered around himself some notion of what dignity meant, walked out to watch Joe at milking time. He nonchalantly marched across the manure-smeared barn floor to get a closer look.

Joe looked up at his curious son and asked Nathan if he might like to try his hand at milking.

Practically ankle deep in manure, the boy proudly lifted his head and declared, "I'm not touching that filthy udder!"

Joe was sad when we eventually had to return the cow to John, but he was glad that he had borrowed a cow before he bought one, for it took Old Red to convince us that farming was not as simple as we had imagined it would be.

Actually, I do not think I had ever really wanted to be a farmer anyway; Joe had. I had wanted to work outside— maybe as a missionary or a marine biologist—but I never saw myself as a modern Laura Ingalls Wilder. The "good old days" had never sounded all that good to me. I did not want to live without indoor plumbing, or my laptop, or my microwave, and I sure was not enamored by visions of having to pluck the feathers off a chicken before I could roast it. No, I would much rather buy the three-pound bag of flash frozen breast fillets and stir fry them just before supper.

So living among a people who had farming in their genes was bound to create some tension in my life. It is not that anyone else said I was supposed to be like them. They did not have to. I put that pressure on myself. By constantly comparing myself to them, I made my own turmoil.

"Becky," said Ruby when I was sharing my heart struggles with her. "You don't have to garden like we do or sew like we do to be one of us. God gave you different gifts. Being Mennonite isn't about having certain skills, it's about being what God wants you to be and using the gifts He gave you to do good in the world."

"It makes so much sense when you say it, Ruby, but I sometimes wish I had been raised like you so I didn't fit in at such an odd angle."

"Well, I suppose we'd all choose to be different if we could, but God has gifted us the way He thought was best, and I'm so glad He made you just the way you are."

Ruby's words were a real balm to me. God had placed me in a Catholic home when I was born. God had seen that I was given the skills He wanted me to have, and God had chosen to not have me grow up in a traditional Mennonite home. Surely God knew what He was doing.

God had also given me a brain that could figure out how to get along in a new culture, and I did not need to be a farmer to find a way to get my hands on some of the finer things the farm has to offer such as home-grown beef.

Joe and I were always on the lookout for places to get good, healthy meat. So Joe was pretty excited when John came up to him some months later with another offer.

"Say, Joe, how would you like a good deal on some naturally-raised, farm-fresh beef?" he asked with another of those sly grins that said, "If you give me your apple, I'll let you paint my fence."

"What's the deal?" asked Joe, now familiar with that particular grin.

"Well, it's like this," offered John. I need to butcher a steer, and he's a bit more than I can handle alone. I thought maybe you and your family would like to try your hand at butchering."

"I'll have to talk to Becky about that one. I'm not sure how well she'd handle butchering. She's got a rule: she'll fix us any meat we bring home, but it better not look anything like an animal."

Joe understood me well. I am not a vegetarian, and I love the thought of fixing healthy, hormone-free meat for my family, but my city upbringing had left me rather squeamish when it came to topics like road kill, butchering, and eating creatures that have names. I was not sure if John's steer had a name, but it surely could have!

Still, I have been known to do some crazy things, and everyone else seemed to think butchering was so normal. Surely I could stand it for one afternoon.

It was horrible. The entire butchering room smelled like blood, and the dust that flew out from the sides of the saw smelled like burning bone (which I guess it was). The meat looked entirely too much like the steer that had glanced up at me on my walk that morning. I stayed with the project until the last bit of hamburger was wrapped in little bags that said "Not for Sale," but I decided that butchering, like gardening, and sewing, is something that was worth paying someone else to do for me!

18

PLOW UP YOUR FALLOW GROUND!

"Plow up your fallow ground! Miracles follow the plow."
Adin Troyer was conducting a series of meetings at Bethany, and his words sliced straight through my heart. If you would have asked me the week before, I would have told you that all was well with my soul: I loved God with all my heart and soul and mind and strength—or at least I thought I did—and I had found a way to comfortably fit into the Mennonite community. I was not chasing after mammon, at least I did not think I was. But the longer Adin spoke, the more I realized that he was talking to me. Somehow, my soul that had once been vibrant and full of Jesus-fruit had grown barren and dry. My spirit had been fallow for a long time, and it had become painfully evident that only a miracle of God could restore the fruit that had once hung heavy there.

How had I come to be so fallow? Was it all the time I had spent trying to be like a thoroughbred Mennonite? Was it the heavy focus on self that such an effort required? Or was it, perhaps, that I had lost my first love and had let the riches of my world choke out the life that had once blossomed in my heart?

I suspected that all of these things had contributed to my sorry condition, but one thing was clear, I needed a heavenly plowing and it was going to hurt.

So many thorns tangle through my story at this point that it may be difficult to separate them into distinct strands that will be visible to a reader, but I will try.

I guess we will need to go back to the time when Colin was a toddler. We were still worshiping at the House of Prayer, and I taught biology and chemistry to the students at their high school.

On a frigid morning in November, I ran out to my car between classes to get something. As I came down the stairs into the parking lot, I noticed that the asphalt was covered with black ice—that almost invisible coating that can jerk the feet out from under the unwary pedestrian.

"Be careful," I said to myself, "this stuff is treacherous." How I could have given myself that mental warning and still stepped out onto the ice as though it were no slicker than dry pavement, I do not know. But I was only thirty years old and still invincible. As I carelessly rounded the rear corner of the car, my feet slipped out from under me and I flew back onto my head. I lost consciousness for a time (nothing unusual there), and when I came to, I picked myself up and went in to continue my day as a teacher.

It did not seem like the tumble had done any real damage until two weeks after the fall I opened my eyes one morning and realized that my left eye had gone nearly blind. My sight was not fuzzy, it was not even black. It just plain was not there. The best way I can describe the missing vision is to compare it to seeing out of the eye in the back of your head. How much can you see from that eye? Why nothing at all of course. You cannot see anything from there because you have no eye in the back of your head. That is how 75% of my left eye had become—it was completely gone!

The fall on the ice had caused me to impact the back of my head so violently that both of my retinas had begun to bleed and detach. I could not see the bleeding at first, so I did not know anything was wrong until two weeks of slow detaching had peeled off enough of the retina to allow me to notice the loss of vision. My right retina was also detaching, but it was occurring so slowly that I had no idea that it, too, was injured until the eye doctor examined me with his slit lamp.

"You will need immediate surgery," he said to me when he finished his examination. "If you delay, you will lose all vision in your left eye. We can wait to repair the right eye until next month."

So I had the left retina repaired. A month later I had the right one repaired. And a few months after that, I underwent another surgery to remove a cataract that had developed in one eye. It was replaced with an artificial lens.

All of this left me with one eye that saw relatively normally and one that saw only very close things. Neither glasses nor contact lenses would allow the two eyes to see together, so I just learned to see out of one eye at a time and tune out the images from the other eye.

My vision had been like this for ten years. Now the strain of constantly tuning out one eye caused me to experience severe pain whenever I tried to look at anything. I began patching both eyes most of the day and cried from the pain whenever I tried to look at the world for more than a few minutes.

That was the state I was in when Adin Troyer came to preach at our revival meetings.

Surely this pain in my eyes was fallow ground. It was not producing anything good that I could see. I was facing a choice between self-enforced blindness or constant pain, and I could not imagine how I would teach my children, or write for CLP, or fix supper if something did not change.

Another weed that had been choking out the fruit that used to be so obvious and plentiful in my soul was my dream to hike the Grand Canyon, preferably with a team of Creation scientists. I would love to see the strata that so clearly mark the layers of flood deposits and touch the fossils that line up in rows as a testimony to the cataclysmic waters that had entombed them those thousands of years ago.

My desire to visit the canyon had become so intense that I had been squirreling away every extra penny from my CLP work in a little drawer. And I already had $1200.

I had another drawer full of brochures and maps about the canyon and all of the wonderful things there are to see in the surrounding area of the United States.

I do not think God minded at all that I was saving for a trip to go see one of the monuments to His Flood, but I do think He objected to the fact that it had become an obsession with me. I thought about the trip with much more intensity than I thought of Him. It had become an idol.

"Plow up your fallow ground!"

I think the deadliest weed in my unfruitful soul though was that I had made being a good Mennonite my spiritual focus. When we had first come to the Valley, it was in response to the call to forsake all and to follow Jesus. But somehow, somewhere, I had lost track of that goal. Instead of being a Mennonite because that was the best way I knew to follow Jesus, I was now trying to be a Mennonite as an end in itself. How had that happened?

"Plow up your fallow ground!" thundered the preacher. "Miracles follow the plow!"

I badly needed a miracle. I needed several miracles. I needed the pain in my eyes to go away. And I needed both eyes to see together. I needed to surrender my dreams of seeing the Grand Canyon, and I needed to stop esteeming the Lord's church above the Lord Himself. I needed to see how to follow Jesus again. I needed to see Jesus.

In tears, I met with my Bethany sisters in the prayer room before the Wednesday evening service and laid my sin and my need before them. They agreed that I was coveting and had lost my spiritual focus. They sweetly admonished that I needed to go to the Lord in repentance and humbly ask Him to take all that was wrong in my life and put it back in focus. They also urged me to take the money I had saved for the canyon and go to an eye specialist.

The irony of the whole situation was that if I kept the money for the trip, I would never really see the canyon, even if I stood directly upon the south rim! My eyes had become unable to see such massive things. But if I surrendered my dream and the money it required, I would not only rid myself of an idol but I might also find a way to see the world again, without pain. The decision was a no-brainer.

The eye specialist had an opening the very next day, and he assured me that he could, indeed, perform a surgery that would bring my two eyes back together again. Hallelujah! And the amount of money that I would need as a deductible, I was told by the deacon, was $1200. $1200! Had he been peeking in my drawer?

I repented of the low position to which I had relegated Jesus and also of the high esteem I had given to achieving some sort of cultural holiness by my own efforts.

In response, God hoed and weeded. He cut and He pruned. But He was really quite gentle about it, and rather than hurting, it brought me peace.

The surgery went very well, and I remember the indescribable joy it was to really behold the mountains that surrounded me. They had contours and ridges that I had never seen before! And I could see my children as they played far off in the fields, and they didn't need little red caps anymore. The sun did not glare in my eyes when I tried to look at the blue Virginia skies. Everything was beautiful, and I could look at it as long as I wanted to; the pain was gone. My own little world was grander than any imaginations I had ever had of the Grand Canyon.

Better still was the joy I felt again in the intimate relationship that had been restored between my Father and me. He was so real again. So big and lovely. So awesome. It was like the days in my childhood when all I had wanted was Him. I hungered and I thirsted and He satisfied my every longing. I was full.

And through all the repenting and the surrendering and the refocusing on God, I was finally able to become truly comfortable with my place in the Mennonite world. I did not have to become anything. I already was.

God in His wisdom had made me exactly who I am, and He had done it just exactly the way He wanted to. I will never be a farmer or a chef or a seamstress. I do not think I will even make a decent pie crust this side of heaven, but I will write and teach and smile and praise with all my heart and may He get all the glory from it.

I will rest secure knowing that the God of the little girl with the sandy, soily rows full of promise, the God of the girl who knew all about the mammon verse, the God of the young mother who left family and culture to walk the Abraham road, the God of the insiders and the God of the outsiders has made me just how he wants me to be: just plain Becky.

Vera's Journey

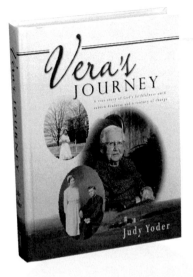

Vera's Journey was almost four years in making and begins in the year 1899. Vera was raised in a divided home. Her mother was Old Order Mennonite. Her father was Dunkard Brethren. At that time the Brethren were very strong on immersion, holding that it was necessary for salvation. These issues caused that Vera said "It was one of the most difficult periods of my life."

Vera was born in 1906, the eldest of five children. She heard the stories of the Great Titanic sinking in 1912. She knew the song of the Titanic. Vera came through two world wars. She suffered with the flu in the great epidemic of 1918 and 1919 when many lost their lives including relatives. In 1933 a son got into his father's medicine and died on the way to the hospital. He was about 17 months old. In 1944 at age 38 she got the mumps. In two or three days she was deaf, stone deaf, never to hear again. After that the family would sometimes find her in the bathroom crying. At other times they would find the towels wet with Mother's tears. Father rallied in support of Mother. When things got too difficult for her, he would say, "Mother let's go for a drive." With her loss of hearing came a constant roaring that she described as sounding like a waterfalls. This noise was with her for the last 64 years of her life. She would never hear her two youngest children cry, laugh, or sing. Vera would often say, "We need to accept what we cannot change."

"At 707 pages, 'Vera's Journey' is extensive but reads like a storybook, rich in description and history, with photos along the way. The book also has an area map, recipe cards, and Ralph and Vera's family trees. 'Vera's Journey' takes a historical look at the matriarch of a Mennonite family living in the [Shenandoah] Valley [of Virginia]."

YODER | 708 PAGES | LAMINATED HARDCOVER | $24.95
ITEM #VER76228 | ISBN9781932676143

• • • To order, please use order form in back of the book.

Stronger Than Pain

This is the story of one woman's triumph over indescribable pain, multiple surgeries and multiple setbacks. Her hospital experiences were in a number of the leading universities of the eastern United States. Arlene's illness was regarded by the medical profession as extremely rare. Highly respected doctors were frustrated in their inability to find answers to this highly unusual case. In the end there were few satisfactory answers.

"Through the years of physical pain and disability, I have prayed many times that God would use me in His service and that He would create in me a heart like Jesus'. But when another cloud of pain strikes, leaving me alone and in darkness, or when I sit looking at the signature line on yet another consent form I find myself asking, 'God, where are You?'" Arlene Kauffman uttered these words that were put into the forward of her book.

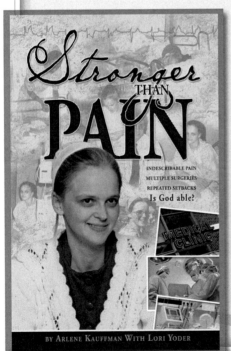

Arlene Kauffman knew pain like most of us can only imagine. Her resolute faith and trust in God to the end is both remarkable and exemplary. This is a wonderful faith building book that is difficult to lay aside.

Arlene's great disappointment was to not be able to tell her father goodbye. She did not know where her wayward father was. This is the story of Matilda Kaufman's daughter who passed away in 2008.

KAUFFMAN | 167 PAGES
PAPERBACK | $8.99

ITEM #STR76174
ISBN9781932676174

To order, please use order form in back of the book.

Shattered dreams

The Heartache and Enduring Hope of a Forsaken Wife

Matilda Kauffman

The heartrending story of one woman's walk that is repeated thousands of times all around the world. Her husband of many years deserted her and their seven children, leaving them penniless.

Matilda tells her story without malice and bitterness. How is that possible? How could she cope? How could she survive? Only by relying on the Lord, Who heard her cry and gave peace to her shattered heart.

Today, she is a living testimony of the healing that comes only through Christ and shows by example how to respond to some very difficult circumstances in life.

Kauffman tells her story with a desire to give hope to other women who find themselves alone, shattered, and betrayed.

A portion of each sale goes toward the support of Matilda Kauffman.

KAUFFMAN | 65 PAGES | PAPERBACK
$7.99
ITEM #SHA76242
ISBN9781932676242

To order,
please use order form in back of the book.

A Woman
by God's Grace

Grace is "the divine influence upon the heart, and its reflection in the life" (Henry). It enables humans to experience and express the characteristics of God Himself. Anna Mary Byler spells out the practical aspects of this life. On page after page, she calls wives and mothers to consider the graces that crown mundane responsibilities with resplendent success and eternal satisfaction.

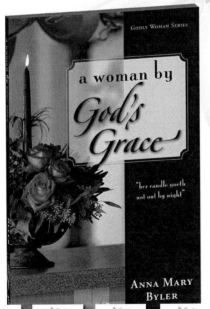

BYLER | 169 PAGES
PAPERBACK
$8.99
ITEM #GRA76129
ISBN9781932676129

To order,
please use order form in back of the book.

Order Form

To order, send this completed order form to:

Vision Publishers
P.O. Box 190
Harrisonburg, VA 22803
Fax: 540-437-1969
E-mail: orders@vision-publishers.com
www.vision-publishers.com

_____   _____
Name   Date

_____   _____
Mailing Address   Phone

_____
City   State   Zip

From Streetlights to Stars Qty. _____ x $9.99 ea. = _____

Vera's Journey Qty. _____ x $24.95 ea. = _____

Stronger Than Pain Qty. _____ x $8.99 ea. = _____

Shattered Dreams Qty. _____ x $7.99 ea. = _____

A Woman by God's Grace Qty. _____ x $8.99 ea. = _____

(Please call for quantity discounts - 877-488-0901)

Price _____

Virginia residents add 5% sales tax _____

Ohio residents add applicable sales tax _____

Shipping & handling ___$4.20___

❑ Check #_____

❑ Money Order   ❑ Visa

❑ MasterCard   ❑ Discover

Grand Total _____

All Payments in US Dollars

Name on Card _____

Card # __|__|__|__| __|__|__|__| __|__|__|__| __|__|__|__|

3-digit code from signature panel __|__|__| Exp. Date __|__|__|__|

Thank you for your order!

For a complete listing of our books request our catalog.
Bookstore inquiries welcome

Order Form

To order, send this completed order form to:

Vision Publishers
P.O. Box 190
Harrisonburg, VA 22803
Fax: 540-437-1969
E-mail: orders@vision-publishers.com
www.vision-publishers.com

_____   _____
Name   Date

_____   _____
Mailing Address   Phone

_____   _____
City   State   Zip

From Streetlights to Stars Qty. _____ x $9.99 ea. = _____

Vera's Journey Qty. _____ x $24.95 ea. = _____

Stronger Than Pain Qty. _____ x $8.99 ea. = _____

Shattered Dreams Qty. _____ x $7.99 ea. = _____

A Woman by God's Grace Qty. _____ x $8.99 ea. = _____

(Please call for quantity discounts - 877-488-0901)

Price _____

Virginia residents add 5% sales tax _____

Ohio residents add applicable sales tax _____

Shipping & handling __$4.20__

❏ Check #_____

❏ Money Order   ❏ Visa

❏ MasterCard   ❏ Discover

Grand Total _____

All Payments in US Dollars

Name on Card _____

Card # _|_|_|_|_| _|_|_|_|_| _|_|_|_|_| _|_|_|_|_|

3-digit code from signature panel _|_|_| Exp. Date _|_|_|_|

Thank you for your order!

For a complete listing of our books request for our catalog.

Bookstore inquiries welcome